Praise for *Who Says?*

"A perfect book for this time. Mechlinski firmly establishes himself as one of the top thought leaders of our era, effortlessly extending his methodology to the reader. This book is not only a must-read but also a must re-read, offering new insights with each encounter."

—Jere Simpson,
CEO of AtlasUP

"*Who Says?* not only asks the right questions but also gives fresh answers. This book challenges readers to embrace the power of having their own true north and honoring it. It gives readers the inspiration and the insight to step out of the herd, listen to your inner voice, and dare to chart an authentic path. You won't find the same old, same old advice. This is a guide—not a template—for anyone who wants to lead with authenticity and until now has felt like they were standing alone on an island trying to do it."

—Gerry Sandusky,
New York Times bestselling author and
voice of the Baltimore Ravens

"Joe is one of those rare individuals with a heart as genuine as his mind is brilliant. Every time I'm around him, I learn something valuable—he has that effect on people. If you're looking for insights that challenge the norm and inspire real change, look no further. Joe is the real deal."

—Garrett Gunderson,
New York Times bestselling author of
Killing Sacred Cows

WHO SAYS?

WHO SAYS?

JOE **MECHLINSKI**

NEW YORK TIMES **BESTSELLING AUTHOR**

WHO SAYS?

QUESTION EVERYTHING, AND *DISCOVER* THE GENIUS OF *THINKING* DIFFERENTLY

WILEY

Published by John Wiley & Sons, Inc., Hoboken, New Jersey.
Published simultaneously in Canada.

For general information on our other products and services or for technical support, please contact our Customer Care Department within the United States at (800) 762-2974, outside the United States at (317) 572-3993 or fax (317) 572-4002.

Wiley also publishes its books in a variety of electronic formats. Some content that appears in print may not be available in electronic formats. For more information about Wiley products, visit our web site at www.wiley.com.

Library of Congress Cataloging-in-Publication Data

Names: Mechlinski, Joe, author.
Title: Who says? : question everything and discover the genuis of thinking differently / Joe Mechlinski.
Description: Hoboken, New Jersey : Wiley, [2025] | Includes bibliographical references and index.
Identifiers: LCCN 2024024139 (print) | LCCN 2024024140 (ebook) | ISBN 9781394265510 (hardback) | ISBN 9781394265534 (adobe pdf) | ISBN 9781394265527 (epub)
Subjects: LCSH: Self-actualization (Psychology) | Creative thinking. | Corporate culture.
Classification: LCC BF637.S4 M435 2025 (print) | LCC BF637.S4 (ebook) | DDC 650.101/9—dc23/eng/20240627
LC record available at https://lccn.loc.gov/2024024139
LC ebook record available at https://lccn.loc.gov/2024024140

Cover Design: Paul McCarthy
Cover Art: © Getty Images | Oxygen

SKY10084459_091324

To my brother Eddie . . .
My heart breaks every day without you here. I miss you hard.
Thank you for being my first best friend, my 24-hour
person, and my North Star.
You always had my back no matter what and taught
me how to always find a way.
You lived life with a warrior spirit and the heart of a lion.
You taught me to be a man with honor, hustle, and heart.
You were an amazing dad, husband, son, brother,
friend, and human being.
This one's for us.

Contents

■ ■ ■

History Is Happening

In the last half-century, we've eclipsed the collective progress of the previous 250,000 years. Consider the journey from rotary phones to smartphones and the evolution from room-sized computers to wearables on our wrists. This whirlwind of transformation means one generation has outpaced the achievements of the last 3,000. Read that again. The velocity of change is breathtaking, yet discerning the difference between the temptations to be resisted and opportunities to be seized remains an ever-growing challenge.

Consider this: advancements in artificial intelligence (AI) are reshaping our reality, and UFO sightings challenge our understanding of the universe. Even our perception of cosmic history is in flux, with revelations suggesting the universe might be twice as old as previously believed.

> "We have Paleolithic emotions, medieval institutions, and god-like technology."
> — E. O. Wilson, Harvard professor and sociobiologist

Work Isn't Working

Here's the good news: the digital era promised a renaissance in the world of work. Then on March 16, 2020, the tables in the workplace flipped. For the first time, humans could work from anywhere on a global scale. The question is, are we ready to be "outdoor cats"?

We spend a third of our waking hours at work. Before the pandemic, more than 70% of the workforce felt disengaged.[1] This disconnect has only deepened, giving rise to the "productivity paradox." Although only 12% of executives believe their teams are productive, a staggering 87% of employees consider themselves highly productive.[2] This gap highlights a growing divide in perceptions and experiences within the workplace.

> "Work is love made visible."
>
> — *Khalil Gibran,* The Prophet

The Future Is Even More Uncertain

History's greatest minds, from Newton to Einstein, were far from right all the time. Our understanding of health, science, and technology is continually evolving, overturning long-held beliefs about diet, medicine, and stress. Fat is good, sunscreen is bad, and we should jump in a cold plunge daily to live longer. At least, this is what we know to be true . . . for now.

> "We drive into the future using only our rearview mirror."
>
> — *Marshall McLuhan*

Here are just a few quotes that, in hindsight, prove that no one knows anything. We are all just making this up moment by moment.

1899
"EVERYTHING THAT CAN BE INVENTED HAS BEEN INVENTED."

— *Attributed to Charles H. Duell, Commissioner,*
US Office of Patents

1903
"THE HORSE IS HERE TO STAY, BUT THE AUTOMOBILE IS ONLY A NOVELTY – A FAD."

— *Horace Rackham, Henry Ford's lawyer*

1932
"THERE IS NOT THE SLIGHTEST INDICATION THAT NUCLEAR ENERGY WILL EVER BE OBTAINABLE. IT WOULD MEAN THAT THE ATOM WOULD HAVE TO BE SHATTERED AT WILL."

— *Albert Einstein*

1962
"WE DON'T LIKE THEIR SOUND, AND GUITAR MUSIC IS ON THE WAY OUT."

— *Decca Recording Co. rejecting The Beatles*

1995
"THE INTERNET? WE ARE NOT INTERESTED IN IT."

— *Bill Gates, Microsoft*

Who Says? is for those who have begun to suspect they've been playing the wrong game: the game of living someone else's life and not your own. It's a book for people who are tired of bad (business and life) advice. And it's a book for those who want to question the unquestionable.

We've all been there, hearing the same rules repeated to us over and over – by your parents, your teachers, your friends, society, and every organization or institution – about what it means to live a good life. This pervasive messaging shapes our perceptions, often leading us down paths that might not align with our truest selves.

A few of us have been lucky enough to find a noble endeavor that makes the world a better place for everyone. But even then, are we truly fulfilling our own desires, or are we simply fulfilling a role set out for us by society?

Most of us, however, get to the end of the journey, cross the finish line, and find ourselves feeling empty inside. This emptiness can be a powerful catalyst for change, prompting us to question the very foundations of our choices and motivations.

You might retire at 65 and finally get a chance to live life on your own terms but find you're too exhausted. This exhaustion is not just physical but often a reflection of a lifetime spent chasing externally imposed goals.

You might sell your company, knowing you got there on the backs of others. You might inherit a lot of wealth from someone else in a way you don't feel you earned or you can be proud of.

We have all had our own versions of moments when we realize we've been playing the wrong game, that, we picked the wrong pill from Morpheus (from the movie *The Matrix*), and we've been deluding ourselves into thinking this life is only about materialism, consumerism, getting more and more for "me."

I want to invite you to join us in peeling back every veil, every layer, of what this whole game is about, specifically where we spend the majority of our time: in the game called *work*. This invitation is about more than just rethinking work; it's about rethinking life and our place in it.

Most of us spend our days racing to a job, to a place. We haven't even considered if it's something we really want to do with our lives. We haven't given ourselves permission to make different choices.

Most books dispensing advice are not hard to find. Success is traditionally viewed as a result of following certain rules and conventions, and these books go to great lengths to codify success. I should know; I wrote two before this one.

Do this to get promoted; do that to get a raise. Do this to be rich; do this to be happy. From dressing a certain way to using specific language to get what you want, we're often taught that sticking to the norm is the best and safest way to succeed.

I firmly believe most of the advice you'll find in these books is useless.

Why? Because human beings can be arrogant as fuck.

The moment we believe we've arrived and found the right way, we become fixated on the path we took as the only path possible – and we begin to tell others this is the right path for everyone.

This fixation can be dangerous, leading us to close off other possibilities and perspectives. I have been the receiver and sender of this type of advice. For those on the receiving end of this advice, it's all too easy to accept as truth.

Whether we like to admit it or not, we're used to being told what to do (and we might even like it that way). We say we want to have full autonomy, but the reality is we are finite beings living in an infinite and eternal universe. It's exhausting, and like a muscle, we need to build our capacity to find what's right for us and only us.

I truly believe most people have good intentions when they first step into leadership or a position of influence. But I think we tend to look at our "influencers" and collectively say "leading" has become

History Is Happening

one big strategic feedback loop focused on seeking an insatiable amount of attention and followers, a continuous cycle of "follow me, look at me."

In other words, too many of our leaders promote their own methods as the best, only to get the attention, validation, and continued "presence" they need to feed the grist. The only thing you are doing by blindly following advice is feeding someone else's ego.

We've moved away from authenticity and slow progress in favor of the instant gratification we get from boasting about our accomplishments online and promoting ourselves endlessly.

Here's the other part of this we're not acknowledging: just because you climbed the mountain yourself doesn't mean you can teach others to do it. Michael Jordan – one of the greatest basketball players of all time – couldn't figure out how to coach.

Greatness in one area doesn't always translate to greatness in teaching or leading others.

High performers like Jordan struggle to unpack their own processes and understand how they might apply (or not apply) to another person. They often rely on signals and signs that work for them but probably are not helpful universally. Recognizing this limitation is key to understanding there's no one-size-fits-all path to success.

So, after "advising" more than 600+ organizations for more than 20+ years, I've learned it's not about finding *the* way, or even finding *a* way, but truly finding *your* way. No one knows you better than you. Everything is situational. Everyone is different.

Although some best practices and guidelines can be helpful, oversimplified processes can suppress our creative impulse and teach us to depend on others to tell us what to do. This ultimately stifles personal growth and self-discovery.

You're probably wondering how the hell I plan to write a book without actually giving advice on well-being. Admittedly, this is a challenge. I think the answer is to share my experiences and the stories and experiences of others, what worked and what didn't work, and the questions we've never been able to answer.

It's an invitation, not a proclamation of *the way* (in my best Mandalorian voice).

This demands a higher level of integrity – no bullshitting you, the reader, into thinking I have all the answers or you're going to finish the book with a 10-step plan in place.

I began writing this book at the start of the pandemic, a time of profound personal and global upheaval. I started with a writing partner with no script, no agenda, no structure, and just a vision for what *Who Says?* was all about.

After many life events, including the death of my college football coach, Jim Margraff; my high school football coach, Roger Wrenn; one of my all-time favorite CEO clients, Pat Murphy; a few dear friends; both our pups of 15 years; and the sudden passing of my brother, Eddie, at age 50, it was time for me to bring this vision and story to life.

Eddie truly embodied this message in this book in his life and gave that gift to me. He was a rebel at heart, always looking to change not just the rules of the game, but the game itself. I will share more about him later in this book.

The time is ripe for a book like this. In the aftermath of the pandemic, many of us are reconsidering how we live, work, and play. The pace – and the pain – of change has never been more intense than it is right now. It makes sense that we revisit the way we spend our days. But it's not just the inflection point of the times we live in that is causing us to question common knowledge. Both research and lived experience are beginning to reveal that blindly following conventional wisdom can hinder progress and potential.

Too often, the best-intentioned advice is the wrong advice.

Who Says? is a collection of personal experiences and counter-intuitive ideas, covering topics from self-actualization to challenging the assumptions of workplace norms. It's about saying what others aren't, exploring the power of personal guidance in the workplace, and challenging readers to rethink their entire human experience.

That in itself is not unusual; however, few folks are talking about the convergence of self-actualization, civilization, dismantling of traditional power structures in the world of work, psychedelic therapy, AI, and yes, even aliens.

And for me . . . this book comes down to this quote:

> "We teach what we need to learn; we create what we need to heal."
>
> — *Richard Bach in his book,* Illusions

Thank you for getting this far and letting me heal. I lay bare my ego, fears and failures, understandings, lessons, heart, and soul.

Peace and Love,

Joe

Introduction

Who Says . . . The Future of Work Can't Be More Human, Not Less?

In 1868, an American inventor Christopher Latham Sholes was granted the world's first patent for a typewriter.[1] There was only one problem: it worked so well that people were typing so fast that it broke all the time. It took him nearly seven years to solve the problem. See, the original keyboard closely mirrored the pattern of letters from A to Z, making it too familiar for the users. Christopher stumbled on the most complex combination we now know as the QWERTY keyboard.

That's right, for the past 150+ years, we have been typing slower . . . not faster . . . on purpose!

This deliberate slowing down in typing speed is a metaphor for how often we are conditioned to operate within limitations, sometimes self-imposed, without questioning their purpose or relevance.

In short, we've been working harder, not smarter.

Talk about another notion we have blindly accepted – *retiring at 65.*

This benchmark wasn't born out of consideration for human well-being or productivity. Its origins can be traced back to the turn of the 20th century in Germany.[2] The chancellor at the time found himself in the throes of a political rivalry, specifically with those over the age of 65. In a strategic move to edge out his competition, he introduced a law mandating retirement at 65, primarily to secure his position in the upcoming election.

This historical tidbit isn't just a quirky fact; it's a profound reminder of how arbitrary decisions and power plays often shape our professional lives.

It raises a critical question: why do we adhere to these benchmarks set for reasons unrelated to our personal growth or happiness? It's a compelling example of how we, as a society, often embrace norms without scrutinizing their origins or relevance to our current context.

That's right. Another notion we think nothing about but should.

But the one that really fires me up, especially as the dad of a 13-year-old daughter and 11-year-old son, is why we have school bells to tell kids when classes start and end.[3]

During the Industrial Revolution, a lot of us worked on factory floors. We were just starting to learn about how to condition behavior to increase productivity. Dr. Ivan Palov's famous experiment with the bell ringing and dogs had just come out. So, the powers that be decided to give it a try with our children. Bells in schools were initially designed to get kids ready to work on the factory floor *and* start them early by blindly accepting things the way they are.

This example is a reflection of how deeply ingrained and unexamined practices can dictate our daily lives, even in education. It stresses the importance of questioning and reevaluating the whys behind our routines and systems.

Why do I know these fun facts?

For the past 20+ years, I have been an entrepreneur, investor, author, advisor, and consultant for more than 600+ companies. After collecting more than 1 million data points (through surveys), do you want to know the number one problem?

Legacy thinking.

Despite what you have been told, the past does not equal the future. *We have always done it this way* is not a good excuse to stop innovating, evolving, and growing.

It's a fact, not a feeling, that we spend the majority of our time at work, and we all know it's broken.

Instead of waiting for the answers from experts like me, it's time to hold a mirror, ask questions, and reflect because the only voice and vote that matters is yours.

Who says how we do things has to stay the same? Not me, and hopefully not you.

So, let's start thinking differently . . .

Who Says . . . Work Has to Suck?

For the past 20 years, we have all heard the challenges:

- Seventy percent of us are not engaged[4]
- Five generations with different values and approaches to work are trying to collaborate and move initiatives forward.
- Mental health and burnout are all headed in the wrong direction.
- Automation and AI are eating half of the workforce.

But for me, I have a very different relationship with "work." See, it literally saved my life.

I grew up in the inner city of Baltimore during the early to mid-1990s. In fact, when you say Baltimore, most people usually "know" it through the HBO show *The Wire*. Despite people's protestations to the contrary and trying to build Baltimore's brand past this popular show, I would say this is a very accurate depiction of my felt and lived experience daily.

Growing up, I went to Patterson High School, which is recognized as the worst high school in the entire state. We started with 965 freshmen and graduated 235 seniors. That's a 23% graduation rate.

I am not just lucky to be one of those 235. I'm also an example that it's not about where you start. You can change your stars. From high school, I went on to graduate and play football at Johns Hopkins University (more on this later).

So, how did I go from one of the worst environments to one of the best environments in the country?

Not legacy thinking, that's for sure. It was my dad. Watching how he approached work literally saved my life.

When my friend's parents, who worked at big manufacturing plants, lost their jobs to automation and offshoring, we were fortunate that he didn't. My dad's job was rough for the first 17 years of his career: hard, blue-collar labor. Freezing in the winter and steamy in the summer. And you want to know what he didn't once do?

Complain. Like at all. Ever.

My life was easy compared to his. And yet, I would often hear him say this to me:

"Joe, I don't have to go to work. I *get* to!"

I get to? I get to work. I get to do performance reviews. I get to pay taxes??

This subtle shift – waking up to your own agency with appreciation – was a major awakening for me. At this moment in time, others are coming to the same realization.

It's a testament to the power of perspective. How we view our work, our choices, and our roles can fundamentally alter our experience of them.

Have you heard of the song by Johnny Paycheck, "Take This Job and Shove It"? Well, apparently, 40+ million people, or one-fifth of the American workforce, joined that movement during the pandemic – the Great Resignation. For me, the Great Resignation felt more like the Great Awakening.

People are awakening to the idea that work is not a have-to anymore. We have a choice. We always have. The pandemic just helped us slow down and see what really matters. Like my dad, we are beginning to listen with our hearts more than our heads and ask, **Is today worth it?**

This shift in perspective, from resignation to awakening, is not just about job satisfaction. It's a larger commentary on how we value our time, our contributions, and, ultimately, our lives.

That's right. Is it worth my actual life? We are thinking about work from a more human perspective, not less, with more heart, not less.

Who says work has to suck? Not me, and hopefully not you. The moment we start questioning these deeply ingrained norms is the moment we start opening doors to a more fulfilling and human-centric world of work.

The second I introduce this "get to" versus "have to" mindset shift to people, they say, "Well, that sounds great, but my boss or company doesn't get it."

Who Says . . . My Company *Won't Change?*

Harvard Business Review reported 70% of change initiatives fail in organizations.[5] Want to know why?

Because we keep thinking work and life are happening to us versus for us.

One of my favorite quotes is "We shape buildings, and then they shape us." If you look at most organizations, they are all shaped the same way – just like almost everything in civilization: a hierarchy, a pyramid. The shape of our structures is a forced function of our culture. This top-down approach, especially in the work world, promotes an adult-child relationship, subjugation, and victimhood.

It makes sense given how we parent and educate . . . and in the work world, it's pervasive. I see this mentality all the time in organizations. But, occasionally, we learn a lesson.

Back to March 16, 2020, when nearly every company made the same decision – to go against every fear-based instinct of letting their people work from home, letting them work from anywhere.

Airbnb let their employees work from anywhere without adjusting pay as a thank-you for their contributions during the pandemic.[6] TowerPaddle Board has been working five-hour days for years now with great success.[7]

We always could have made these decisions. These options were always available. What other options are we leaving on the table?

The future of work is in your hands. Your voice and vote matter. Do you want Friday off? Let's all make the decision and find a way to make it work.

It all starts with a simple question: *who says?*

The best way to predict the future is to create it. Let's cocreate this next version of work together. And to me, it starts with questions, not answers. Sounds personal, right? Well . . .

Who Says . . . Work and Business Are Not Personal?

How many times have you heard "it's just business, it's not personal"?

If we go back a couple of hundred years, before the Industrial Revolution, marketplaces and business would only happen one afternoon a week.

Thursday afternoon was "market day." Everybody would get dressed up in their Sunday best and go to the market. It was an environment you didn't want to get too wrapped up in because it was full of snake oil salespeople shouting out exaggerated claims.

Everybody had the best of everything to sell and applied persuasive tactics to convince you. Persuasion and manipulation eclipsed truthfulness and honesty in the marketplace. At the end of the day, everybody would go home, not thinking about money or transactions for the rest of the week. After the Industrial Revolution and with the advent of factories, we became able to produce things in much larger quantities, and then we needed to sell them.

Today, some shops are open seven days a week, and the marketplace is active 24/7 with the internet. We are glued to devices that continuously shout advertising slogans at us and never let us escape the marketplace. We live permanently trapped in a transactional mindset.

The win-at-all-costs mentality is finally starting to crack. The idea that human nature is to transact with each other is not our natural state. Business is personal because it's our life.

This is not a new conversation. In 2017, Google published its findings from Project Aristotle, where it studied hundreds of teams to understand the main driver of a high-performing environment.[8]

The number one driver is psychological safety, not a pressure cooker. In an environment where people feel seen, safe, and supported, they ultimately feel like the team has their back. Sounds pretty personal to me.

Growing up on the streets, I can tell you there is no better feeling than having friends who have your back and will literally lie down in traffic or take a bullet for you.

There is an actual human on the other side of the computer screen. They have a story you know little about. The next chapter of the workplace can easily unfold with more humanity, not less.

Who Says . . . You Need a Personal Legacy?

Are we here to spread ideas and change the world? Most people think of personal legacy as putting our name on buildings, statues, and organizations.

But how about the example of MIT? Everybody has heard of the prestigious Massachusetts Institute of Technology, but very few people have heard of William Barton Rogers, who founded it in 1861. It was not named *Rogers Institute*, and so it was free to assume a living identity of its own.

And how about TED? Most people know this site, home to tens of thousands of inspirational ideas and talks, but many have no idea of its founder, Richard Saul Wurman.

Legacy is not what you do but what you help others to do.

I lost my mom when I was 23. She passed tragically at 44. Every day I get is a day she does not. It's a gift. Some would look at this as tragic, and there is a version of me that feels that. But what she helped me do is her legacy.

She was an amazing lady. Spiritual. Creative. Theatrical. Loving.

This is her legacy.

Today, I am here with you because of her sacrifices, sharing how we can bring more heart and humanity to the future of work and really consider where we spend all of our time.

I am her legacy.

I invite you to consider – as we did on March 16, 2020, when we collectively decided to work from home on a dime out of fear – that we can today, out of love, collectively play a different game.

A game where we are not victims of circumstances. But rather have an attitude of gratitude. A game where we are not using business as the reason to treat each other as less human but rather we remember we are all brothers and sisters on this rock hurtling through the universe. It is a game in which we are not focused on winning only for our own glory. Instead, we see each day and moment as an opportunity to plant a sequoia tree for the collective.

Like my parents did.

As we tackle the next series of challenges with automation, hybrid work, and mental health, the message is simple: double down on yourself and each other. Bringing heart and humanity to the future of work is not easy, but it is worth it.

And, in the end, it's time to flip the script from who says? . . . to **what say you?**

Chapter 1

A Life of Disruption

"In order to save myself, I must first destroy the me I was told to be."

— The Dreamer

Part 1: Original Tracks: The Song in Your Heart

My parents met when my dad, Jim, pulled his van over to pick up a hitchhiker, my mom, Debbie, while back from California, where she had been living out her dreams of becoming an actress.

It was love at first sight.

In less than six months, they tied the knot, and three months later, I was born.

Because my parents were both young, I ended up living with my grandparents until I was five in a very tough neighborhood. Eventually, I made my way back to live out the rest of my childhood with my mom and saw my dad on the weekends. He was never short on love but was always short on time. However, he never missed a major moment that mattered to me.

As a single mom with little money, growing up in the worst parts of Baltimore City, my mom did her best to hold onto a sense of purpose and teach me the lessons of life along the way. We were poor, which meant we slept on other people's couches often. I went to five schools in five years. Because my mom was diabetic, she was constantly struggling with her health, in and out of the hospital, and unable to keep a steady job, which caused us to not have enough to eat and unable to pay the bills. She tried to work, but then she would get sick, lose her job, find another job, and then get sick again.

Lacking access to basic human necessities like food and shelter was the hardest thing to deal with for me and my mom, too.

I always found myself curious about other people's lives and what they were like. People appeared happy because they had choices, money, and resources. One of the greatest gifts my parents gave me was teaching me to have enough of a sense of pride and to know I didn't want to live life as a charity case or live on food stamps forever.

Let me tell you a story . . .

At 11 years old, I was living on the second floor of a small row-home with my mother – two bedrooms, a bathroom, and a very small kitchen.

The musty, unclean apartment reeked of smoke. There were two empty cartons of cigarettes in the trash, and brown butts of various shades filled the ashtray that sat on the small, second-hand coffee table in front of the couch. Next to it were water rings from my mother's ever-present Diet Coke. Once, I made the mistake of taking a sip from her glass – not Coke! I was woozy the rest of the afternoon.

I remember straightening up the apartment and making her bed at home by myself. The summer heat was stifling as the apartment didn't have air conditioning. Realizing I was hungry, I went to the kitchen and opened the refrigerator.

Inside was an old carton of milk, mostly empty and past its expiration date, a jar of mayonnaise with about two teaspoons left, and an uncovered pot of macaroni and cheese from the night before. Some wilted fruits and veggies were in the drawer, and an opened stick of butter was on the side door. One bottle of Diet Coke is half empty, and there are lots of insulin bottles and needles.

Slamming the door quickly, I close my eyes and begin to imagine food in the refrigerator. I'd heard time and time again from my mom about the power of thought from the books she was reading by authors such as Wayne Dyer and Shirley McClain.

"If you just believe strongly enough, you have the power to create your own reality; you just have to want it badly enough."

So, I asked, wished, nearly begged, pleading out loud for food, edible food.

My tiny hand pulled open the door, hoping it worked – nope.

Just then, I heard a thud. I knew instantly it was the weekly church delivery of food to people like us, people who needed help. Maybe my plan worked!

I ran to the door to find a brown grocery bag on the threshold with food abundantly falling out of it. Inside were pasta noodles, a can of tomato sauce, macaroni and cheese, peanut butter, and jelly. At the bottom was a small loaf of bread, half smashed by the food on top of it, and a whole slab of butter. Systematically organizing everything where it was supposed to go, I was now marveling at the cabinet and shelves, now filled with plenty.

These deliveries felt the same as Christmas morning at my grand-parents' house, waking up to gifts under the tree.

Just then, my mom's voice called to me as she always does when she comes home. She's wearing black leggings, an oversized sweat-shirt, and beat-up tennis shoes that used to be white. A black purse over her right shoulder with things falling out of it. She's 27, five-foot-three, and 100 pounds soaking wet.

"Where's the bag from the church, Joey?" she calls out. "Did they deliver it?"

"Yes," I answer quietly. I'm already feeling a sense of where this is headed.

"Did you look into it?"

"Yes," I admit, also in a low tone.

"Where's all the stuff?"

"I put it all away already."

Immediately, I was upset that I hadn't hidden some of the food from her. Even at the young age of 11, I had already learned to with-hold and lie, as I had learned too many times the lessons of what having excess meant to my mom.

"Look, Ma, pasta and sauce, peanut butter and jelly, and it's not even generic!"

Her eyes light up. We are laughing together, enjoying this rare moment of enoughness.

She looks away, out of the window, as if she's in deep thought. In a matter of seconds, she smiles and says, "You know what? I have an idea."

I definitely should've hidden some food.

She starts looking through the cabinet, "Let's take a look at what we have and figure out what we can give away. We don't need to keep all of it."

I feel a burning sensation in my chest. I'm distraught. Mad. Furious.

Before I know it, we are on our way to deliver our "excess" to another family with several children to feed. Seeing and feeling their gratitude gave me a chance to feel something I had forgotten.

The anger dissipated as I took her hand and whispered, "This is what life's about. It's not about what you get; it's about what you give and who you have helped."

"That's my boy," she says with a proud smile.

That day could have built up resentment in me, but giving that food away felt like finding the truest version of myself. Similar to a warm blanket – comfy and cozy, it felt right. It felt counterintuitive because we were going against society's idea of the "right way to be poor" by refusing to cling to the little we had and, instead, sharing it with others.

It set up a lifelong habit of giving myself permission to think differently and change the rules under any circumstance. It taught me that living aligned with a higher purpose was way more fulfilling than living in fear and lack.

Most important, listening to your heart's song will rarely steer you wrong, but going along with someone else's cover song will.

A Life of Disruption

Part 2: What Game Are You Playing?

I am a space geek. I've eagerly followed every development and new knowledge about the universe, from the iconic images captured by the Hubble Telescope to the more recent, awe-inspiring glimpses from the James Webb Space Telescope, positioned a million miles from earth.

The Netflix documentary *Unknown: Cosmic Time Machine* sheds light on our cosmic history and the incredible journey of this telescope.[1] What's interesting to note is the documentary opens with a line about the age of the universe: 13.8 billion years.

Just three weeks after the documentary's release, a significant finding by Rajendra Gupta, a physics professor at the University of Ottawa, challenged long-held beliefs. His research indicates the universe is double the age, approximately 26.7 billion years, we've been taught it was.[2]

This begs the question: if our understanding of something as fundamental as the age of the universe can be off by a staggering 13 billion years, *what else might we be missing?*

What do we think we know?

What do we know that we don't know?

And what don't we know (that we should know) that we don't know?

We've been taught what we should know versus how to think. We have been taught to pursue the answers versus the questions.

Research by the Office of Economic Opportunity for NASA's Imaginative Thinking Test found we are 96% less creative as adults than we were as children.[3]

As leaders – especially when it's crunch time and the pressure cooker is turned up – how often are we just looking for the answer versus focusing on the quality of the questions we're asking?

We see this movie play out all the time: an executive has a problem and is only interested in the quick fix. A perfect (and recent) example of this is a CEO who came to my company frustrated by his team's lack of performance and losing their top salesperson.

His request was for us to design a new plan for his executive team. Can we do that? Sure. Is that the right approach? Not even close.

He's starting with the answer – not the question – as to why there's a lack of performance and why his top performer "unexpectedly" quit.

Jumping to the conclusion that compensation will fix the problem, he doesn't even wonder what the real problem is. This helps no one. We can blame this on many factors, but one place to look is how we've been taught to think.

Divergent thinking versus convergent thinking boils down to whether you start with the question or the answer.

Convergent thinking starts with the answer and then finds facts to support the answer, whereas divergent thinking starts with a question that initiates ideas. The only place we get to when we start with the answer instead of a question is right where we started. Figure 1.1 illustrates the modes of thinking.

Have You Heard of the Marshmallow Challenge?

The Marshmallow Challenge involves teams who are given 20 sticks of spaghetti, one yard of tape, one yard of string, and a marshmallow. The task? Build the tallest free-standing structure with the marshmallow on top within 18 minutes. Sounds easy, right? Here's where it gets interesting: kids consistently outperform adults in this challenge.

Why do kids do better than adults?

- Embracing experimentation:
  - Kids approach the challenge with a sense of play and experimentation. They're not afraid to try multiple iterations, learning and adapting as they go. Adults, however, often spend too much time planning and less time doing, which can limit their ability to adapt and improve.

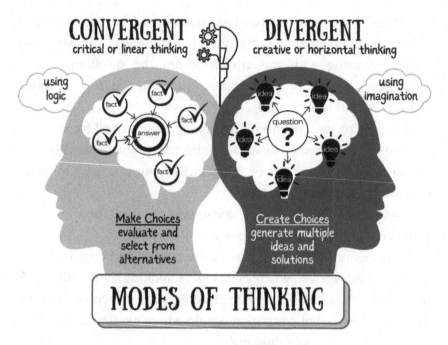

Figure 1.1 Modes of Thinking

- Lack of assumptions:
  - Children don't come into the challenge with preconceived notions about how things should be done. They are open to all possibilities and are willing to try unconventional approaches. Adults often bring their biases and assumptions, which can hinder creativity and innovation.

- Collaboration over hierarchy:
  - Kids work together more fluidly, sharing ideas and building off each other's contributions without worrying about roles or hierarchy. Adults often fall into structured roles and might struggle with collaboration, leading to less cohesive teamwork.

- Focus on the goal:
  - Children keep their eye on the prize – the marshmallow on top. They remain focused on the end goal, while adults can get bogged down in the process and details, losing sight of the ultimate objective.

The Marshmallow Challenge highlights a crucial lesson: innovation thrives in an environment where experimentation, open-mindedness, and collaborative spirit are encouraged. It's also where lateral thinking, the convergence of divergent ideas, happens and real breakthroughs can occur.

What Say You? Questioning Convention

Did you know the average adult asks six questions a day compared to the average kid who asks 125? What are the questions you have always wanted the answers to?

Here are a few of mine:

- Are we alone?
- What's life all about?
- Where did all of this come from?
- What happened before the Big Bang?
- How can we live in abundance without money?

What are yours?

Why do these questions matter to you, and how have they influenced your thinking or actions?

■ ■ ■

Most of us have heard this story before:

A young woman is preparing a roast for dinner, and, as her grandmother did, she cuts off the ends of the roast before placing it in a square pan to cook. One day, her partner asks her why she cut off the roast's ends. She replies she's not sure, but it's how her grandmother always did it.

Curious, she calls her grandmother to ask about the reason behind this practice. Her grandmother laughs and explains she only cut the ends off because her roasting pan was too small to fit the whole roast.

Although the story may be a fictional example, there are indeed real-world traditions participants follow without fully understanding their origins or purpose. These practices often continue for generations, becoming ingrained in the culture. Here are a few examples from around the world:

- **The Baby-Jumping Festival (El Colacho) in Spain:** This unusual tradition involves men dressed as devils jumping over infants to cleanse them of original sin.[4]

- **The Bullet Ant Initiation in Brazil:** The Satere-Mawe tribe in Brazil has a coming-of-age ritual involving young men wearing gloves filled with bullet ants, whose bites are among the most painful in the world. The purpose is to prove one's strength and endurance.[5]

- **The Aghori Sadhus in India:** The Aghori are known for their extreme and unorthodox rituals, like meditating over corpses or consuming human remains, as a path to enlightenment.[6]

- **The Tomatina Festival in Spain:** In Buñol, Spain, participants engage in a massive tomato fight each year. Although it's a fun and popular event, most don't know its origins: it involved a spontaneous food fight among villagers in the 1940s.[7]

- **Firewalking in Greece:** In some Greek Orthodox communities, many partake in the tradition of firewalking as a cultural tradition, with no understanding of it being an ancient practice with deep spiritual significance.[8]

These examples show how traditions can persist in cultures even when their original meanings or purposes have become obscured over time. Participants often continue these practices out of a sense of cultural identity, community bonding, or simply because *"it's always been done this way."*

We live in a world full of senseless traditions and routines: wearing neckties, tying shoelaces, and setting off fireworks in the middle of summer. These are all things we've learned to accept as normal, even though they make no sense on deeper reflection.

We print trillions of dollars to fund sophisticated weapons designed to kill people on the other side of the globe whom we have never met, and yet we don't have the resources to address the housing crisis or to feed people experiencing poverty.

We work our whole lives before "retiring" to finally get the chance to do what we really wanted to be doing all along.

We celebrate Thanksgiving when there is little debate now that this was not a happy time between the Indigenous people and the Europeans.

We freely give our attention to smartphones when we are aware of the predatory profiteering involved and that it would be much healthier to be outdoors or talking with loved ones.

Even the idea of national borders only makes sense to one of the 5.3 million species on this planet. It's as if to say, "This is my country, and here's a little piece of paper called a passport. Now, whenever you want to walk across this imaginary line, you will need to show this paper I printed to a random person in a made-up costume called a uniform."

Yet, for an extraordinarily small group, fewer than 600 people throughout history, there's been a glimpse beyond this constructed reality, achieved by venturing into space.

This unique experience, known as the *overview effect*, offers an entirely different perspective on earth.[9] From this extraordinary vantage point, the planet is not segmented by borders or marred by conflicts. Instead, it presents itself as a cohesive, vibrant entity. The usual lines that divide us – our nationalities, racial differences, and economic inequalities – dissolve, revealing an earth unmarked by such divisions.

The striking beauty and apparent fragility of our world become evident, with its blues and greens shining against the vastness of space. This view also highlights the thin atmospheric layer that cocoons the planet, a frail shield against the void of space, emphasizing our planet's vulnerability and our duty to protect it.

This shift in viewpoint urges us to rethink our priorities and the artificial divisions we impose. It invites us to acknowledge our collective duty to safeguard the delicate balance of our unique planet.

It's weird, right?

There are so many strange things we do together, and yet so many of us go along with it all without ever asking, "Who says we have to do things this way?"

Nowhere is any of this truer than in the workplace.

Before the COVID-19 pandemic, a great majority of the world's population was willing to get up unusually early in the morning, wear uncomfortable clothes they might not usually wear in a relaxed environment, drive a long way in stop-and-go traffic, and then sit in an uncomfortable air-conditioned office without natural light where they generally did not feel they could really be themselves.

A "workday" often involves eating food you wouldn't usually eat under rushed circumstances, and then, at the end of a long day, driving home again and spending time on evenings and weekends trying to recover from the whole unpleasant experience.

The same people who were willing to drive long distances to unwelcoming environments became "pencil pushers," moving forward an agenda they may not completely understand or that may not resonate with them and about which they were never consulted in the first place.

The option to work remotely gave many of us the opportunity to reflect on the limited choices we had previously been required or allowed to make. Everything we had taken for granted about work was thrown up in the air, enabling many timely questions to come into focus: "Who makes the rules around here? Who says it has to be this way?"

Of course, opting out of a broken system to live on savings, in a van, or your parent's basement is a very temporary solution and an option with a lot of privilege attached. We need to create new systems in which no one is obliged to participate against their will, but rather, we are invited to cocreate.

What Say You? Doing Your Own Thing

When I was in high school, my teachers, with the best of intent, tried to discourage me from applying to Johns Hopkins University. I was not the caliber to get into Hopkins, so maybe I should focus on a community college instead.

The same was said when I started my first business at 19. Although my friends and family warned me not to do it, I grew it to 150 people in three years, while still in college.

At 23 years old, I began playing with the idea of starting SHIFT (the company I run today), but the traditional guidance showed up again, which was to get a job first, learn how it's done, and then do my own thing.

Whether we absorb these discouragements from others or apply them ourselves, without a nearly rebellious attitude, we might concede and not try, because of the pressure that "it's always been done this way."

What's a time you have been discouraged by others or have discouraged yourself in the name of because "it's always been done this way?"

Did you go with the advice, or did you chart your own path? What was the impact?

A Life of Disruption

Miki Agrawal is the author of the book *Disrupt-Her*. She is a serial entrepreneur who had already taken on several different industries and turned them on their heads before she reached the age of 40.[10]

When working in the movie industry in Los Angeles, she was struck by how the catered lunches provided on set seemed unhealthy and indigestible to many of the cast. She returned to Brooklyn and opened a revolutionary new pizza chain, using gluten-free crusts, heaps of fresh vegetables, and non-dairy cheeses.

But she didn't stop there.

Aware that every menstrual product on the market had been developed by men, she created Thinx, an absorbent underwear which allows people much greater freedom to get on with their life while having their period. She went on to found Tushy, a bidet attachment for your toilet to solve for the issues caused by using dry toilet paper. This kind of thinking is obvious once presented to us, but it takes asking disruptive questions.

And to ask disruptive questions, you need a disruptive mindset, one that challenges the established societal ways, preconceptions, and belief structures. And, in addition to the questions and challenges, a disrupter also has to come up with a solution and take action.

A contextual disrupter is someone who looks behind the picture, at the back of the picture, or what's in the corner of the picture.

The reward of looking at things in a fresh way can be enormous. But there's a big downside to being disruptive in that you're going to get crucified. Jesus was a disrupter. Galileo, Martin Luther King Jr., John F. Kennedy – you can just keep naming them. People get run out of town or killed.

Most people operate in the world as if it is a conveyor belt. Same thing day in and day out. Disrupters see the world differently. They see infinite possibilities all the time and instead of taking steps 1 through 10, step-by-step, they figure out how to go straight from 1 to 10. This is why disrupters often become entrepreneurs: because they're simply unemployable.

The History of Disruption

It has always taken disruptive thinking to take us in a new direction. Because of the emergence of factories during the Industrial Revolution in London, everyone was moving from rural areas toward the bigger cities to find work. This was before the invention of the motorcar, and London was getting buried every day under mountains of horse manure and thousands of gallons of urine. A headline in *The Times* of London in 1894 announced that "in 50 years, every street in London will be buried under nine feet of manure."[11]

No one could see any way out of this until Henry Ford popularized the internal combustion engine with the Model T Ford. Of course, this has created a whole bunch of other environmental problems we have had to deal with since, but the point is, Ford did not try to address the problem of what to do with the horse manure directly. He questioned the underlying assumption about what is essential to transportation.

In his book *Enlightenment Now*, Steven Pinker points to the extraordinary progress that has been made in the last 200 years – exponential, relative to any other time period in recorded history.[12]

At the same time, we are challenged to face more unsustainable facets of how we live together on this planet than ever before – an imbalance of equity and income, climate change, the impact of technology on mental health, and a healthcare industry that has lost its heart and is losing its workers. Compared to 200 years ago, 95% of the world no longer lives in poverty.[13]

Many well-intentioned companies do everything they can to improve the quality of life for their employees. Some put the most up-to-date, luxurious gym on the premises. Some bigger Silicon Valley tech companies have installed restaurants on campus that serve organic food, on-site massage, acupuncture, or meditation pods.

As long as we are still operating in a context where people are going to work because they have to – because they have gone so far into debt – we are still using bandages rather than addressing the underlying problem.

People are only going to work because they feel they "have to" rather than "wanting to" because they feel inspired.

A Life of Meaning and Purpose

In dozens of interviews with disruptive thinkers, they all talk about having a bigger purpose. It's not about just challenging the status quo for the sake of it, but doing so for the betterment of humanity, to leave the world a better place.

In *The Second Mountain*, David Brooks talks about how we as people try to climb the first mountain of fame and fortune, and if, or when, we get there, we realize the second mountain is about the fulfillment of purpose and impact and service.[14]

The first mountain is what society tells us to chase: the fame, the fortune, the whole nine yards. We hustle, grind, and sometimes, we even make it to the top. But here's the kicker – once we're up there, looking down at all we've achieved, there's this nagging feeling. Is this it?

Then there's the second mountain, which isn't what the world sees as success. It's about purpose, about making an impact, about serving others. Heart and soul over ego. This is where fulfillment lives, connections are made, and communities are built. It's about digging into who we are and transforming who we are to find our place in this big, crazy world. It's about *we*, not *me*, and it's a journey worth taking.

If people with a lot of pain and suffering can transmute that into purpose, we change the world. Through my mom's example, I climbed the second mountain first, and through my own healing, forgiveness, and grace, I have tried to inspire others to do the same and let them know it's possible.

It Ain't Easy

Questioning things as they have been presented to you is not easy. It requires tremendous commitment and support from others who also see things in this way.

> "A person's success in life can usually be measured by the number of uncomfortable conversations he or she is willing to have."
>
> — *Tim Ferriss, author & innovator*

Thinking and living disruptively reignites our lives with inspiration, energy, and purpose, and requires tremendous dedication. That's why most people don't do it. People don't reflect on how they think and act because that takes a lot of time and energy. You need to have a very compelling reason to stop the music and ask why? or who says? There's also a fine line between having disruptive thinking and being so disruptive that you get stuck and unable to move forward.

Those who rely on the outside world for a sense of safety will never think disruptively, because "safe" is easier, it feels better. The fear of being shunned, of being disliked, excluded, othered, or ultimately killed, will keep you playing within unexamined assumptions.

There's some truth to the old adage, *"Easy choice, hard life. Hard choice, easy life."* We as human beings avoid the hard stuff. We avoid adversity even though it can be an ally.

Adversity helps us figure out the hidden capabilities to pressure test the best and brightest ideas, build competency, and see we're capable of the impossible if we can just put our minds to it. It also teaches us who our real friends are.

Change is hard and we humans resist it. And although we know it's for the better, we also know better isn't always easy.

Finding *Your* Way

One of my biggest mentors and muses, and someone I consider a friend, is Richard Saul Wurman, founder of TED and author of 91 books. He is one of the biggest disruptive thinkers I've met. He has lived his life for an audience of one, himself. Richard has told me over and over again that every one of his 91 books was for him, not the audience. Are you trying to *be* good . . . or *look* good?

I have had the privilege of learning from his life's work, which both this next quote and the fable shown in Figure 1.2 could sum up.

"The most essential prerequisite to understanding is to admit you don't understand."
— *Richard Saul Wurman, founder of TED, author*

UNDERSTANDING UNDERSTANDING BY RICHARD SAUL WURMAN

A **dot** went for a walk and turned into a line.

It was so excited by this that it jumped up and down on its tip and did a dance. It twirled, looped and turned somersaults in the air until it became a **drawing.**

The **drawing**, all scrambled up in the sky, squealed for hours and turned into a cloud of **song**. The song took a step and became a **dance**, improvised yet formal, expressing a wide range of emotions, like a **tango.**

The **notes** of the **song** that fueled the dance morphed into **words.** The **words** formed groups and then found **meaning.** When **words** and **meaning** held hands, they formed a **story,** which is a **map in time.**

The **meaning** turned from **words** to **pictures** and found itself on the walls of a dark cave and the mysterious cavity that resides in all of our heads. The **dot,** the **line,** the **dance,** the **notes,** the **story,** the **song,** and the **meaning** all embraced and formed **memory.**

Emboldened, the **dot** took a walk and came to a fork in the road. A sign on the left read looking good and behind the sign, the dot saw all manner of rewards and awards - all aesthetically pleasing and beautiful things. It didn't quite understand what it saw, but it was certainly seduced.

The **dot** looked to the right and saw a sign simply saying, being good.

After seeing all these things that looked beautiful, it saw something quite different - a world of being good, a world of understanding, a world of good work and accomplishments.

The **dot** quickly made a choice between looking good or being good, and headed towards the right fork.

At the end of the road of being good; the **dot** found out it was just a handshake and a hairbreadth from looking good. By being good, one naturally becomes beautiful, gains meaning, memory, and purpose.

The **dot** walked on to find another fork in the road. A sign at the left said, big data. The sign was good and intricately made. On the right, the sign - quite minimalistic and with clear letters - read big understanding.

Big data or big understanding - the choice is simple, the goal clear.

The **dot**, the **line**, the **dance,** the **story,** and the **painting** had found **connection. Memory** became **learning**; learning became **understanding.**

LEARNING IS REMEMBERING WHAT ONE IS INTERESTED IN. LEARNING, INTEREST AND MEMORY ARE THE TANGO OF UNDERSTANDING.

Creating a **map** of meaning between data and understanding is the transformation of big data into big understanding.

THE DOT HAD EMBRACED UNDERSTANDING. UNDERSTANDING PRECEDES ACTION.

EACH OF US IS A DOT ON A JOURNEY.

Figure 1.2 The dot

Source: With Permission from Richard Saul Wurman and inspired by Paul Klee.[15]

■ ■ ■

People want to make a difference in their lives. This is what everyone longs for more than anything. I've been with people in Africa who had no shelter, but their primary commitment was to make a difference in their lives. People will give up anything to make a difference in their lives. If they get just a whiff of what it means to live a life that matters, a life of contribution, then it doesn't have to be self-sacrificing when you give things up. On the contrary, it's fulfilling. You sacrifice nothing, and you gain everything.

Ultimately, a life of disruption is both fulfilling and challenging. It is the hardest mountain to climb, but it also offers the most spectacular views. In order to find enough motivation to shift our life in this way, we first need to reawaken our own innate values, our reason for being alive, accessed from deep within ourselves.

I call this *true north (your uni-verse).*

What Say You? The 25 Reasons Why: Navigating a Life of Disruption

As we land the plane for Chapter 1, I want to share and invite reflection on "the 25 reasons why," one of the most significant exercises I've used for over two decades to guide individuals toward uncovering the real purpose behind their choices (see Figure 1.3).

In short, is what you are doing *really* worth it?

I stumbled on this reflection when I started to question everything back in the early 2000s, spurred by the low graduation rates in Baltimore's inner-city schools, which I was a product of.

In response, I cofounded b4students with a vision to weave the business community with the educational landscape, aiming to broaden students' horizons through corporate mentorship. Our ambition was to transform mentorship, making tangible impacts on students' futures.

A compelling example of the impact of our efforts is seen in the story of a young aspiring chef, a student within the b4students program. Tasked with articulating 25 reasons why he wished to pursue a career in culinary arts, his initial reasons were superficial: money, material possessions, and social status.

25 REASONS WHY

UNDERSTANDING THE "WHY" FOR WHAT YOU DO

OVERVIEW

You want to understand how your passions play into your work. 25 Reasons Why is an exercise to help you uncover the top reasons why you do what you do. The first 10 reasons you list will likely be specific to you (the things that bring you joy); numbers 11 to 20 are often connected to others in your life; and the final 5 reasons typically connect to a higher purpose or solving for a societal need (the altruistic nature within).

HOW TO

List out the 25 reasons why you do what you do. This is open-ended and should be completed in a creative, quiet space that allows you to thoughtfully reflect. Once you're finished, circle your top three reasons. This is where your passions truly lie!

1.
2.
3.
4.
5.
6.
7.
8.
9.
10.
11.
12.
13.
14.
15.
16.
17.
18.
19.
20.
21.
22.
23.
24.
25.

25
REASONS WHY

Figure 1.3 The 25 reasons why

However, as he dug deeper, his true passions emerged – service, creativity, the joy of nourishing others, and the desire to honor his grandmother's sacrifices by caring for her in her old age. His journey from superficial goals to uncovering profound, personal motivations highlights the transformative power of introspection.

Since then, we have used this exercise with no less than 10,000 business leaders, and it rarely disappoints.

Here is an invitation for reflection:

- **Reflect on your path:** Use "the 25 reasons why" to explore the true motivations behind your career choices. List them out, one at a time. Then, circle the most resonant reasons.

- **Explore your organization's purpose:** Extend the exercise to understand your company's core mission and values. These insights are crucial for building a narrative that genuinely resonates.

- **Narrate your personal journey:** Merge your individual why with your story, sharing it to inspire and connect with others.

- **Craft your company's story:** Weave your organization's why into a narrative that clearly communicates your mission and vision.

How can you start incorporating these resonant reasons into your daily actions and decisions?

Embracing a life of disruption means valuing the stories we tell ourselves as much as those we share with others. Through "the 25 reasons why," you can find your true soul's purpose for what you are doing and with whom.

Chapter 2

Your Uni-verse

"Don't just teach your children to read . . . teach them to question what they read. Teach them to question everything."

— George Carlin

Part 1: Changing My Stars

Do you know what it's like to win the lottery? I do.

Growing up with unconditional love but without the basic necessities is an odd dichotomy. Deep down inside I knew things would be okay, but the roller coaster of circumstances would oftentimes get the best of me. It was weird to not have enough clothes to get through the week or enough money to pay for food at the grocery store, yet still hold onto the belief that anything is possible, which was instilled in me by my mom (Debbie), stepmom (Rose), and dad (Jim).

Life felt unfair.

The feeling of scarcity and lack was an undercurrent of everyday life. There was always an inner battle at play of "enoughness" – not *having* enough, which often led to not *feeling like I was* enough. This not-enoughness took me to the darkest places inside of myself later in life, but it also propelled me to achieve *no matter the circumstances*.

After attending five schools in five years, I began my journey at Patterson High School and it was instantly clear to me that sports, academics, and extracurricular activities were going to be the only way through and possibly my only way out.

Luckily for me, I had a brother named Eddie who showed me the way in the streets and on the field. Although I had already done the things that "made me a man" by 13 years old – Eddie's guidance and unique way of toughening me up was one of the key reasons I didn't just make it out of Patterson alive but actually thrived.

To say I excelled in those four years would be an understatement. I became a standout athlete in football and lacrosse, MVP and lacrosse team captain as a sophomore, all metro and all-state honors in football, where we were ranked number one in the state for the majority of the year. Outside of sports, I was class president, volunteered regularly, and was selected for a national honor band for playing the drums.

This was all while the school was dealing with real problems like police showing up often to deal with fighting among the students both inside and outside of the school. In fact, to stop the flow of students coming into the school, they would padlock the doors, much to the chagrin of the fire department. Imagine: a school that could hold 2,000 students with all but a handful of doors not padlocked.

Drugs, violence, and gangs were a consistent force at Patterson in the early to mid-1990s in Baltimore City. The halls smelled of marijuana and burnt hair, which was from the growing problem of students setting fire to each other.

As much as this school was a living hell, it was "my home," and I became the elected spokesperson by my peers to deal with the issues. During my junior year, the state of Maryland got involved to take over the school and privatize it. In response, I led a group of students to walk out in protest, not having any idea of what was really going on, other than we didn't want to be "taken over" by some foreign invader.

We fit every stereotype of an urban school you could imagine. We had tremendous real-world problems, struggled in academics, but thrived in sports.

Football was our crowning jewel. When I arrived at Patterson, it was on the heels of our quarterback being shot, and it thrust one of the very best athletes I have ever played sports with, Willie McGirt, into the spotlight.

We won the Baltimore City Championship three years in a row, and even made a run for state our senior year before being bested by one of the top all-around high schools in the state.

Our track record was because of our athleticism as individuals and as a team, but more so was because of our heart and hustle. We were all acutely aware that getting a scholarship was the ticket out of the streets. Being recruited and getting an opportunity meant everything and we played like it.

Each year the National Football Foundation and College Hall of Fame hosts a program where one student from each high school is invited to a dinner to determine who is worthy of the prestigious scholar-athlete award. A coveted award in the high school football scene. Winning was a huge deal, one that caught the attention of local news and newspapers (pre-internet days!).

I will never forget the day my football coach, Roger Wrenn, told me he wanted to nominate me. He asked me a series of questions about my grades (which was a 4.0 GPA), extracurricular activities like band, volunteering, and being class president.

Side note: I was 5'8," 175 lbs., middle linebacker and center. Yes, read that again. I was fast, also strong, but short. I would lift weights during the school day and even after every practice. I even benched 325 lbs. my senior year of high school, which at the time broke our school record.

Coach went on to ask me about my life before high school. He dug into how I attended a new school every year, helped my sick mom as she suffered from diabetes, lived without the basic necessities, and experienced constant instability. As I answered his questions, he looked at me and said, "Wow. You are the finest scholar athlete I have ever nominated."

He even wrote this in his letter of recommendation, which I still have to this day.

Of course, I was thrilled Coach "saw me," but what stuck with me was that it was the first time where I could "see me." All the effort and struggle, the setbacks and lack, the not-enoughness, and the fear I had endured seemed like it was worth it. A sliver of hope shined through as I began to see that I might have a chance to break free from the circumstances I was in and live life on my own terms.

The event was at this fancy facility in Baltimore, the nicest place I had ever been to at this point in my life. Without a formal jacket to wear, I borrowed one from my friend Nick, along with a pair of slacks that didn't fit well. Right before the event started, one of the assistant coaches, Coach Lewis, noticed how nervous I was and how uncomfortable I felt. We made small talk about how nice we both had cleaned up. I complimented him on his tie, and he shared with me it was his good luck tie and if I won, I could have it.

Walking in and seeing all of the other scholar-athletes while reading their stories and accomplishments, I went from feeling like I was a big deal to a "nobody" quickly. It was that same feeling of scarcity, lack, and not-enoughness I had when walking into the grocery store hungry without money.

Coaches, parents, sports announcers, recruiters, and athletes filled the room – 500+ people. As nervous as I was and as insecure as I felt, I sized up all the other competition from Baltimore City. Although the other scholar-athletes were impressive, I had this tingly feeling inside that there was a shot I could win the region, which was a big deal because it came with a small scholarship.

After two hours of introducing each nominee, it was time to announce the winners. Of course, of the five regions, Baltimore City was last.

If you are not from Baltimore City, it's hard to understand how people look at you when you say it's your hometown, much less go to one of the inner-city schools there. It's a mix of surprise and feeling sorry for you all at the same time.

Finally, the announcer said, the winner from Baltimore City is . . . *"Joe Mechlinski from Patterson High School."*

The feeling I had when my name left the man's lips is something I can still feel today.

I made my way to the stage, clapping and beaming with pride as tears filled my eyes.

My acceptance speech was a few jumbled words of "thank you" to my parents and my coach as I held the "dish" in my hands, I felt appreciation. Appreciation for myself – all my sacrifices, hard work, late nights, early mornings, and the extra effort that made the difference and clearly paid off.

Having spent the last few years breaking the cycle of not enough, this win was a surge to my heart and a boost to my confidence.

As I made my way back to my seat, I wondered for a second if I had a chance to win the overall award. I was up against Bobby Sabelhaus – an all-metro, all-state, and Gatorade Player of the Year for the entire country. He already had a full ride to play quarterback at the University of Florida, while I was hoping to merely catch a look from a D3 school somewhere.

I wondered if I could manifest it to happen and found myself talking to God. If he allowed this to happen, I would be forever grateful and would continue to work hard so I could create the life I wanted. Even though I believed the probability was low and this would be a winning lottery ticket moment, I sealed my negotiation with God and surrendered that this was Bobby's moment, and not mine.

The names of the winners for each region were announced again along with their accomplishments, and then I heard, *"And the winner for this year's 1995 National Football Foundation and College Hall of Fame for the entire state of Maryland is . . . from Patterson High School, Joe Mechlinski."*

What the fuck just happened? Did I just win? Did he make a mistake? Do I get up?

The whole crowd went nuts, and everyone jumped to their feet, cheering and clapping. I saw my dad and Rose – their faces were beaming as if it was the best night of their life. I looked around, and it was as if it was all in slow motion, with the roar from the crowd coming in and out of my ears while everyone's eyes were on me.

In shock, still seated in my chair, I felt the elbow from the guy next to me as he told me to stand up.

As I stood on stage, the lights were so bright I could barely see the faces but could feel the energy. I humbly accepted the award, and the words that made the way out of my mouth went something like *"I want to congratulate all the other scholar-athletes, and I'm honored to just be among them."*

Coach Lewis rushed to me with his tie half off and handed it to me as we both hugged and cried. I still have that tie to this day. The other players and coaches surrounded me with high-fives, fist bumps, and words of congratulations. And finally, I got to hug my dad and Rose as a moment of guilt hit me, missing my mom as she was in the hospital with another complication from her diabetes.

From that moment forward, I could feel a tailwind behind me.

My picture was taken with all the other athletes, and as the media went to interview me, the big question now is, you have won this award from the NFL and College Hall of Fame – *where do you want to go to college?*

Without any idea as to why, I blurted out, "Johns Hopkins University."

Little did I know, the football coach from Johns Hopkins was in the crowd.

The story of the poor kid from Baltimore City winning this award was a big deal, but even more so because the last Baltimore City kid who took the overall award was Kurt Schmoke, the beloved mayor of Baltimore City at the time.

The mayor invited my parents and me for a photo op at City Hall. More articles in the newspaper – all the moments were surreal and also felt right.

Your Uni-verse

The poor kid from Patterson High was off to Hopkins, which was a story the community latched on to. However, I still had a big challenge, which was my SAT score. After taking the test five times, my highest score was 1000, and I needed 1400 to get into Hopkins.

Being the first in my family to go to college, we had little clue about how the process worked. Coming from an academically weak school, I didn't know how to study for tests and had never written a paper. A few of my teachers from Patterson would listen to me talk and help me write my essays.

"To be successful in life, you must first surround yourself with people who want you to succeed." My dad gifted me this nugget of wisdom, and it's one I live by even today.

Then one morning, I got the call that changed everything. It was Ritchie Schell, the football coach from Hopkins, who said, *"Boy, are you ready to change your life and come to Hopkins?"*

To which I answered, *"Hell, yeah!"*

This quantum leap was one of the most significant moments in my life. It helped me see that I could change my stars by listening to what was in my heart and following my true north. It was hardly a straight line or easy path, but one that was well worth every single moment of struggle.

Part 2: True North

In the previous chapter, we reflected on a life of disruption, one in which we question commonplace assumptions that no longer serve us. I acknowledged how challenging it can be to live this way because we can feel adrift in an endless ocean without direction. When you are clear on your purpose and where you're headed, it's easier to challenge unexplored assumptions.

Because it requires taking a strong stand to think disruptively and to live a life of deep meaning and purpose, we need to be able to sense and connect with our own deepest innate values. I call this *true north*. Imagine you are sailing from Tripoli on the south shores of the Mediterranean to Sicily. It's a distance of a few hundred miles, and it requires sailing north (see Figure 2.1).

As you might know, if you've ever been in a sailboat, you can't always be pointing in the direction of your destination. Under such circumstances, because of the prevailing winds, you need to engage your sail with the winds, to go a little bit to the left, a little bit to the right, a little to the left, a little to the right, all the time keeping your compass and the North Star as a reference for where you want to end up.

The North Star is a guiding principle, it's not a destination. Obviously, you're not trying to sail to the North Star; you're not imagining you're going to land your boat on a distant sun 430 light years away. The North Star defines a direction around which other decisions will make sense.

Each and every chapter of this book is a guide point to help you access your own North Star and deeply trust what you discover. Until you have a sense of your own innate values, that elusive deepest inner knowing, and you know what your ideals are, it is going to be difficult to know what to do next and how to align with other people with integrity.

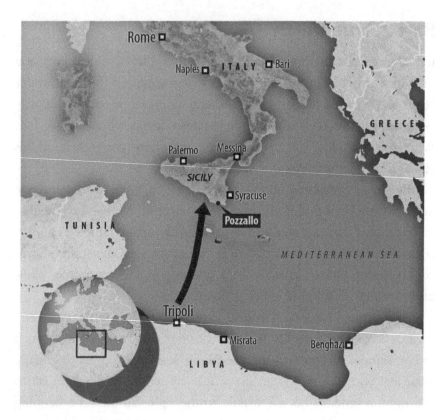

Figure 2.1 True north

What Say You? Your Values

What are the values that you would never compromise, even in the face of adversity? Reflect on situations where you've had to make tough choices. How did these values guide your decisions?

-
-
-

•

•

Describe a scenario where your values were tested. What were the consequences, and how did it shape your understanding of this value?

■ ■ ■

Being guided by values is true for everybody within an organization, not just the founder or the CEO. Even if you are working in the mailroom, as a janitor, or in a call center, everyone needs to have their own true north to be able to make good decisions about what to align with and to feel a sense of meaning and purpose.

In 1962, amidst the fervor of the space race, President John F. Kennedy's speech at Rice University captured the nation's imagination with the bold proclamation, "We are going to the moon." This declaration has resonated through history as a beacon of ambition and American ingenuity. However, a less known yet equally poignant moment occurred as Kennedy was exiting the venue. A janitor, holding the door open for the president, exchanged greetings with him. When Kennedy inquired about the janitor's role at the university, the man replied, "I'm here to put a man on the moon!"

Back to the sailing analogy: remember, your boat will rarely be facing in the direction of your final destination. Although you want to go north eventually, at any particular moment, you will find yourself pointing northeast, northwest, northeast, northwest. A life of disruption is exactly like that. We each have to discover the relationship between long-term vision and short-term strategy: the balance of idealism and pragmatism.

Ever wondered why the US can't agree on our basic history? In his comedy special, *Where Was I*, Trevor Noah nailed the differences between the US and Germany in this way. In Germany, they teach their kids about Hitler without guilt but with the responsibility that now that they know, it can never happen again.

Once we establish true north and relax into our values and ideals, we can ask ourselves what small corrective measures we can take tomorrow, this week, and this month to start moving in the direction of true north.

Life is complex. We are rarely faced with simple, clear decisions that can be made relative to one simple set of priorities. In fact, we find ourselves constantly in conflict between opposing sets of values. *I want to work hard and create a good quality of life and financial security for my family.*

This might require working long hours. *I also want to be there for each and every Little League game. I want to take good care of myself so I don't show up stressed with the people important to me. Oh, and I also want to have fun and enjoy life.*

Day-to-day decisions become difficult because we feel like we always have to choose among conflicting priorities.

Back in the 1970s, people like Gregory Bateson and R. D. Lang researched what happens to people when they are presented with multiple confusing and conflicting narratives; much of their research is based on families.[1] This kind of "double bind," where it is impossible to make a clear decision about what to do next because of conflicting messages and information, creates a "schizoid" state in the psyche and will cause one to feel crazy.

From working with leaders in many fields, I have discovered this schism between idealism and pragmatism can be truly painful.

As a result, we often numb our potential connection with true north and say to ourselves, "Screw it. I'm just going to do what I have to do. I'm going to get mine." We may also move in the other direction and align so inflexibly with idealistic values that we lose our connection to day-to-day life. Then things don't work for us in a material way.

Take Pat Murphy, my dear friend, client, and the late CEO of John Hancock, as a prime example of a leader who struck the right balance. Pat's journey from humble beginnings to leading a major corporation is a testament to staying true to one's roots. He had this unique ability to hold onto what was right, keeping calm when everyone else was in chaos, and ensuring the ethical choice was always made.

Leading an organization of more than 2,000 people, especially in the cutthroat realm of corporate America, is no small feat. But Pat had a knack for not sweating the small stuff. He even kept a compass and telescope on his desk – symbols of his approach to leadership. They were constant reminders to stay focused on the bigger picture and enable that vision to guide his decisions.

I remember a particular instance when he was able to apply his philosophy to a tough situation. The board of directors was pushing for more cost cuts, and Pat's response was grounded in his straightforward philosophy: *"There are only two things in life you can control: your attitude and your effort."* This mindset enabled him to navigate the complexities of running such a large company where he was accountable to stakeholders that weren't always aligned with him.

Living in the space between idealism and pragmatism, maintaining sight of your true north while adapting to the shifting winds of reality, is a challenging yet vital balance to achieve. It's about steering your course through life's unpredictable waters, finding a path that's true to your values and feasible in practice.

Your Uni-verse: The Song You Were Meant to Sing

Stephen Cope's *The Great Work of Your Life*[2] is a compelling exploration of finding one's true calling or *dharma*, as termed in the Bhagavad Gita, an ancient Indian scripture. Cope investigates the lives of influential figures like Ralph Waldo Emerson, illuminating how they discovered and pursued their unique paths, providing us with valuable insights into finding our own.

The poem shown in Figure 2.2 was hanging on the front of my fridge in my Mom's handwriting.

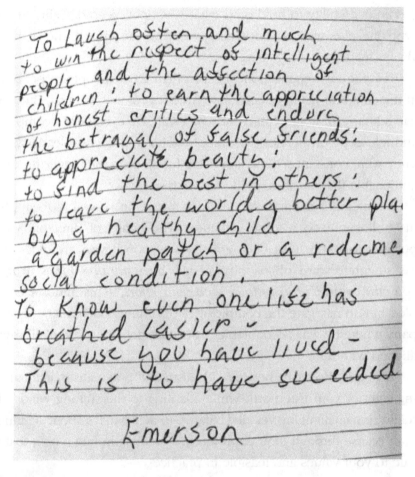

Figure 2.2   Emerson poem

An inspirational example of individualism and self-reliance, Emerson's journey highlights the importance of trusting our inner voice and convictions, even in the face of societal pressures and norms. Cope uses Emerson's life to exemplify how aligning with our inner truths can not only lead to personal fulfillment but also make a significant impact on the world. Emerson's legacy teaches us that the path to finding our "song" – our unique contribution to the universe – often requires courage to diverge from conventional routes and embrace our authentic selves.

Cope's book serves as a reminder that each of us has a unique gift to offer, a specific role to play in the grand tapestry of life. It encourages introspection and mindfulness, urging us to consider our passions, strengths, and values, and how these can be harnessed to serve both our personal growth and the greater good.

The key takeaway is that by embracing our true nature and dedicating ourselves to what genuinely resonates with us, we not only find our song but also contribute to the harmony of the universe. This journey is not just about self-discovery but also about making a meaningful and lasting impact in the world.

We Each Carry a Sliver of the Great Mosaic

As we grow older, most of us learn we need each other. We discover no one individual can have a complete vision of true north on their own because each and every one of us has a vision that is myopic because we are all living within our own personal simulations.

If you want to unfold a truly holistic vision for an organization, this might not be achieved by electing one leader who knows better than everyone else – because that leader will also have a myopic view. Instead, maybe it's through a creative organizational design where everyone is encouraged to take the time to connect with their own true north and share it, generously.

If we flatten the triangle of power within the organization and turn it into a network of nodes, where insight, as well as course correction, can come from anywhere within the system, we'll discover that the organizational true north is almost always something cocreated rather than imposed by one individual.

A Chorus of Voices

It can be painful and discouraging when you realize the ways you have been living day-to-day are out of alignment with your personal true north. When we have supported leaders in organizations, we notice this is often reflected in the use of language analogous to mental illness. "Yeah, I'm really busy at the moment. My calendar is packed. It's kind of crazy, really. Been jamming this week. Super busy – it's insane." We throw these words out liberally to indicate a kind of intensity. But the words *crazy* and *insane* are actually synonyms for psychosis.

It's time to think like Audrey Tang, Taiwan's trailblazing digital affairs minister.[3] She's not just safeguarding democracy against the dark side of artificial intelligence; she's flipping the script and using it to power up the democratic process. Alignment Assemblies, her brainchild in collaboration with the Collective Intelligence Project, is a type of online forum for citizens who are diving into big questions on ethics, impact, and other hot topics, guided by a ChatGPT-like chatbot. It's democracy going digital, making sure everyone's voice is more than just a whisper in the wind.

When working with leaders, we often hear them say things that translate to "My life is so busy that really only someone suffering from mental illness would allow themselves to get this out of balance."

This state of being should immediately trigger a slowdown, fewer hours working and more time for reflection in order to bring the person back into alignment with their own innate values.

What Say You? How to Find True North

Because we have all lived most of our lives in social systems that are exogenous, the first step in supporting any leader, or indeed anyone working anywhere within an organization, is to take steps toward reconnecting with a sense of true north that is truly yours, not borrowed from or inspired by someone else.

Lynne Twist said once, "Look for the global problems that really upset you, that you think are unfair. There's a clue there. Look at the people you admire . . . the things that you have committed yourself to over and over again . . . What is your stand? Why were you born? What are you here for? What is your life really, really about?"[4]

I love these questions she asked, though:

- What breaks your heart?
- What makes your heart sing?

This kind of work, re-enlivening core, innate values for everyone within an organization, needs to be deep and thorough, not just window dressing. For that reason, we're not going to pretend we can get there by reading this book. But what is realistic is taking a small step forward by going through a few simple exercises.

The Future Self

True north, our vision of how things could and should be, is often fully intact but has been disowned as part of "the future." It is easy to bypass this compartmentalization with a simple framing exercise of writing a letter to your future self.

Here is a letter I wrote to my 90-year-old self:

Dear 90-year-old Me,

It's me, writing to you on the eve of my 46th birthday.

I hope this letter finds you in amazing health, surrounded by love, and overflowing with joy.

My biggest hope for you is that you lived life to the fullest to your heart and soul.

That you gave everything you had, held nothing back, and lived a life of service and contribution that left a positive impact on the world.

That you lived your calling, your sense of purpose, and your greatest dharma with a zest for the little moments in life.

You were fair, and fun to be around, and you took care of many while many took care of you.

You were a great friend to many . . . and many right back at you.

You had their back, and they had yours.

That you led with love and always took the high road, especially when it was hardest.

You loved life and everything in it with your whole self, not just your spare.

You moved the big needle and made a difference.

You grew regardless and shifted the work, turning Who Says? into a movement of What Say You?!

Suffering helped you understand how to serve and that you spoke truth to power, always remaining humble and wise.

You were a warrior in a garden.

You lived every day from the heart, helped raise great humans, & built a life w/ Erica as a "we."

Erica is still the best part of your day, and your love has deepened to an unimaginable level.

You witnessed Ellie and James listening and following the unique songs of their heart.

They were part of the greatest work of your life.

Your legacy is not what you did but how you helped others.

You honored those lost in stories.

You traveled the world in distance and depth of the human experience.

You explored the depths of your consciousness and the cosmos.

You played a role in progress, used your heart and art to create unique expressions of your soul, and faced your deepest fears with courage.

You did what you came to do. You lived In truth, In love.

You also fit in a little surfing, hiking, writing, playing, acting, painting, building, and teaching.

Making your own music and marching to your own beat.

Now, as a 90-year-old, I hope you are still mobile, agile in mind, body, and spirit, still make Erica belly laugh, and still hold hands and take walks. There is nothing you can't do together.

I hope you are far from done creating and adventuring and that you continue to mentor and be mentored.

Question everything with ease and grace, and live with a gentle wisdom that continues to see more of how things work while always knowing you know very little.

It's been a wild ride, but remember, the best is ALWAYS yet to come.

Take care, and I'll see you soon.

Love, Me

P.S. – And remember, the universe only gave you what you could handle . . . you always found a way, just keep going!

What say you? How might this read for you?

Your Obituary

When we look back on the past, it may appear like a straight line: one thing happened after another. But the future is not like that; it is an endless series of crossroads with multiple possibilities at each decision point. Once a choice has been made, each crossroad will open up a whole new set of possibilities that would not have been available through any of the other choices.

Consequently, it is possible to imagine a future of no regret, one in which every decision is made aligned with true north. If you were to live in this way, you would die with no regrets.

Speaking of, *The Top Five Regrets of Dying* is one of my favorite all-time books.[5] It was written by Bronnie Ware, a palliative care nurse, who interviewed more than 1,000 people at the end of their lives and found these to be the most common regrets.

I think about them often.

1. "I wish I'd had the courage to live a life true to myself, not the life others expected of me."
2. "I wish I hadn't worked so hard."
3. "I wish I'd had the courage to express my feelings."
4. "I wish I had stayed in touch with my friends."
5. "I wish I had let myself be happier."

In his book, *The Power of Regret*, Dan Pink highlights the transformative power of regret through the interesting story of Alfred Nobel.[6]

Imagine Nobel's shock when he read his own obituary, mistakenly published due to his brother's death! This obituary, far from praising him, labeled him the "Merchant of Death" for inventing dynamite. Confronted with this harsh legacy, Nobel experienced deep regret. However, he didn't dismiss this emotion; instead, he used it as a force for change.

Determined to redefine his legacy, Nobel ultimately bequeathed most of his fortune to establish the Nobel Prize, honoring significant contributions to humanity. This act of philanthropy completely altered how the world remembers him – not as a harbinger of death, but as a benefactor of mankind. Pink's recounting of this story serves as a powerful reminder: regret, if embraced and acted on, can be a catalyst for profound personal transformation and a tool for shaping one's legacy.

Imagine what the people gathering at your memorial service might say about your life or the obituary that would be written.

What would be most prominently emphasized in a life of no regret?

"Eventually all our graves go unvisited."
— *Conan O'Brien*

In 100 Years

This is a great way to uncover the values of true north, not just for individuals but also for teams. When we think about how we want things to be one year from now, it's generally almost entirely dictated by pragmatism: what is possible given the countless constraints and is only minorly influenced by idealism. If we throw the ball further up the playing field five years from now, the practical constraints will become a little looser and the vision a little stronger. In 10 years, 20 years, 30 years – this continues to be true. There is a dramatic jump, however, when we imagine a future in which we will almost certainly no longer be alive. If you think about how you would like the world to be 100 years from now, that vision is likely to be devoid of self-interest and totally determined by what you wish for future generations.

My company has frequently conducted this experiment with leadership teams. Not only does the vision become more of an expression of core values as we move into the future but it also becomes more aligned among members of the team. If you ask a group of people where they would like the company to be a year from now, there might be a lot of disagreement. When you ask them to envision the way they would like to see the company in 100 years, it is extraordinary how much their visions will align.

As you uncover a clear articulation of an ideal future in 100 years, for an individual or a team, it is then possible to start to align short-term decisions (even if only a small percentage of those decisions) with the values of extremely long-term vision.

Before Your Mother Met Your Father

Now we're getting a little into woo-woo territory, but hey . . . whatever works, right?

If you're looking for a bit of inspiration, check out Taylor Sheridan's *1883*. It's probably the first story shared truly about the grit, resilience, and raw human spirit of pioneers. This series, a prequel to the popular *Yellowstone*, doesn't just portray the Old West's challenges; it dives into the deeper aspects of human decision-making and perseverance against all odds. It's a narrative that echoes across generations, reminding us of our roots, struggles, and that the legacies we inherit profoundly shape our own journeys. Watching it might just provide a fresh perspective on how our ancestors' choices and circumstances are intertwined with our own paths and the decisions we face today.

Think back to a decision you made approximately 10 years ago. Can you see how in certain ways, you are still dealing with the consequences of that decision today? Whether that decision was wise or unwise, almost everyone says yes.

Now, go back 20 years. Can you see how you are still dealing with the consequences of decisions from the past, whether positive or negative? Do the same with a decision you made when you were a teenager or even as a small child.

Now imagine, just for a moment, as a wild flight of fancy, the night when your mother and father conceived you. Go back to a few moments before. Even though no one knows for sure, can you imagine that you somehow existed even then but without a human body? Could there have been a moment of looking down and deciding to take human form?

Becoming a human being involves all kinds of unpleasantness and inconvenience: bellyaches, taxes, betrayal, heartbreak, sickness. Faced with such a perilous landscape, you have to have a pretty good reason to be a human being, particularly at this time in our collective history. If you just took a wild guess, what do you think that motivation might have been for you before you were the you in a human body? What was the driving force that motivated the decision to take human form?

Of course, for many people, this method is a bit of a long shot because most have no idea whether or not they existed before conception. But, if there is even a vague instinct of this, it can be an excellent way to reconnect with the core values that drive your human life, and even as a leap of pure fantasy, it might help you connect more deeply with a sense of mission and purpose.

Role Models

We all have people we admire and respect. Often, these are the people who took a stand with their lives – Martin Luther King Jr., Rosa Parks, John F. Kennedy, or Nelson Mandela. These are all people who have changed the trajectory of history; they were committed not just to change but to transformation, and they lived this commitment every day. It can be a powerful exercise to think of a few of your most important role models and write down the specific qualities they had that you admired. The kind of values you admire in role models are a great clue to your own personal sense of true north.

If I had to point to one area in my life that has been a driving force in changing my stars, it's with mentors. People who stepped up and in to help me for no other reason than they saw something in me that I didn't see in myself.

Allow me to share a few with gratitude: my brother, Eddie; Ms. Flater; Mr. Watkins; Roger Wrenn; Stan Burns; Tony Pasco; Jim Margraff; Jason Pappas; Derek Coburn; Brian Le Gette; Jeff Cherry; Steve Lishansky; and Richard Saul Wurman all played significant roles in my journey thus far.

List your top five role models and the specific qualities you admire in them. How can you embody these qualities in your own life?

What Would You Do If You Had $100 Million?

A very common reason why people abandon true north and get lost in the hustle is the thought that they need to make more money to survive. Survival fear becomes a driver long after it remains logical, even when you have millions in assets and hundreds of thousands in annual income. A good way to bypass this preoccupation with day-to-day survival is to contemplate how you would live your life if you inherited several million dollars or won the lottery.

Of course, many people initially imagine a life of indulgence: going on cruises, playing golf, or lying in bed all day watching movies. Let's probe a little deeper. Most of us can be honest enough with ourselves to realize that a life of pure indulgence would quickly get boring. If we project such a fantasy a little further into the future, it can be a great way to reconnect with core values. There are specific methods to do this in a more structured way known as *time-line therapy*.

> "I think everybody should get rich and famous and do everything they ever dreamed of so they can see that it's not the answer."
>
> — *Jim Carey*

Get Support

It is incredibly important to remember how challenging it can be to live in alignment with your core values. Just about everything in the outer environment, especially in the world of work and organizations, is attempting to pull you out of yourself and your innate core values and encourage you to cooperate with other people's agenda. For this reason, it is almost impossible to do this alone. You need support.

I have interviewed dozens and dozens of disrupter thinkers for this book, and pretty much all of them were actively engaged in a coaching relationship primarily because you get objective feedback. A good coach encourages you to ask questions, to create mental movement in your own brain, to see the world a little differently, to challenge assumptions, and to remove the barriers that are inhibiting you from living your fullest potential.

Identify someone you can mentor or seek mentorship from. How can this relationship help you or them align more closely with core values?

■ ■ ■

In Chapter 3, we will dig into the one core assumption that underlies almost everything that gets in the way of reaching the full potential in the workplace, whether it be an individual's or organization's full potential.

In every interview I conducted, I asked people to contemplate this question: "What's the one thing that everyone knows is true, but isn't willing to say?" And, sometimes to my surprise, pretty much everyone came to the same conclusion.

Chapter 3

Power Over and Under

"The day the power of love overrules the love of power, the world will know peace."

— Mahatma Gandhi

Part 1: You Don't Belong Here

The first day at Johns Hopkins University felt like stepping into a world where I didn't belong. The historic campus buildings stood tall, embodying centuries of academic excellence, and on the inside, I was like most new college students – terrified and excited all at once.

To make the case more bluntly, I couldn't hold anything on either side of my digestive tract for the first two weeks of football camp. I was a literal mess.

Football was one thing, but the academic rigor was a whole other universe.

Choosing my courses was the first real test of my independence. The university's course catalog was an overwhelming maze of complex titles and descriptions like Macroeconomic Theory and Organic Chemistry.

Having never really written a structured academic paper or read a book from cover to cover, I decided to face my weakness of writing head-on and signed up for Principles of Literary Criticism.

The first assignment was straightforward: write a five-page paper on *Madame Bovary*. A relatively simple task for most, but this was a monumental one for me. Not only was I filled with paralyzing anxiety but I also was short on time as I juggled my daily routine of going to class, football practice, studying late into the night, and worrying about my sick mom in the hospital.

A few days after submitting my paper, my professor asked to see me. I entered her office with a naive hopefulness, only to have it shattered within minutes.

"Have you ever written a paper before?" she asked sharply.

I answered, "Well sort of . . ."

She looked at me, confused and slightly irritated.

"Are you pledging a fraternity?" she asked.

I said, "No," equally confused, but starting to feel uneasy.

She asked me straight, "How did you get here?"

It was a moment where I wanted to let my guard down and trust the world would be kind and fair. I wanted to start fresh with my story at Hopkins, so I began to share with her my story of becoming.

I told her about Patterson, the award, my sports background, a little about my mother, and then she interrupted me and quickly spiraled into an interrogation of my academic legitimacy as she concluded, "I don't think you belong here."

Her words, a punch in the gut, sent me through a gamut of emotions. Initially anger and then doubt and insecurity, wondering if she was right that I didn't belong.

Although I felt underestimated, unseen, and questioned whether or not I was an imposter, her words ignited a fire inside of me to keep going and reject any notion that her opinion would define my truth or destiny.

My salvation came in an unexpected form – my roommate, Dan Gigler, one of the future editors of the *Pittsburgh Gazette*, along with a group of supportive friends. They became my lifeline community, helping me navigate the complexities of academic writing and providing the encouragement I desperately needed.

Despite the odds, I passed the class, which was a victory over my own doubts and fears and a testament to my resilience and determination. Meant as a dismissal, the professor's words, "You don't belong here," became a challenge to rise up.

And rising up meant doing it my own way, not contorting myself to fit into preconceived molds and expectations of others. I wanted to carve out my own space, even in environments that discouraged me from doing so.

This would not be the only time I would hear these words at Hopkins.

Every term paper, final, or test, became an existential battle of me versus the world at Hopkins.

I mapped out the very best path to 120 credits. I avoided the truly hard classes, found friends to help me with tests, and got a hold of old back papers and tests.

Another dear friend, Chris Gaito, would become my study partner the night before every big exam. His willingness to slow down and help me during those all-nighters is a big core memory.

Throughout the experience, I am not sure I ever felt safe enough to take a deep breath to settle and sit into the experience. Johns Hopkins became more than just a university for me; it was a battleground where I learned the true meaning of resilience, self-belief, and the power of defying the odds.

A microcosm of a larger struggle to find one's place in a world that is quick to judge and slow to understand, my time at Hopkins taught me that true belonging comes from within, from a deep sense of self-worth and the courage to be authentic. This experience shaped not just my academic career but also my entire approach to life and work.

I'll never forget that moment in the professor's office.

In fact, from that day forward, I never told anyone about my background and story entirely. I didn't want to get found out. I didn't want the rug pulled.

It stuck with me in every challenge and in every environment where I've felt out of place. It taught me who I am and where I belong is defined by me, not by others.

The true test of belonging is not in conforming to the world, but in having the courage to allow the world to conform to you. To anyone who's ever felt like they don't belong, know this: your unique journey, your struggle, and your perspective are your strengths, not your weaknesses.

Embrace them, and you'll find you belong anywhere you choose to be.

Part 2: The Power Inside

Despite the trillions of dollars pumped into companies to fix disengagement at work, 70% of people continue to go through their days without any sense of meaning or purpose.[1]

Have you ever been asked, "What would you do if you inherited a lot of money or won the lottery?" One of the most common answers is, "I would quit my job."

If you dig into what that means, something is disturbing and deeply sad about that answer. It illustrates how so many of us are spending our days doing things we definitely wouldn't do, if we just had money.

The same is true about retirement. We work our entire lives looking forward to getting the golden handshake so we can stop working and do the things that are actually meaningful to us. And by the time we get there, some of us are too tired to do the things we waited our whole lives to do.

There is a painful schism between what people would ideally like to be doing in a perfect universe and the compromises they have to make by "getting a job" and "earning a living."

For most people, especially the 70% disengaged, work is a "have to" not a "want to."

It Is All About Power

In writing this book, I talked to dozens of the world's leading experts in organizational development and leadership, asking everyone some variation of this question: "What aspects of the workplace contribute to this persistent lack of engagement?"

The uniformity of the answers was surprising and can be summed up as follows: the issue of disengagement isn't necessarily in the job itself, but rather in the inevitable power imbalance that comes with how organizations are structured and what they invest in.

It's adult to child. We tell grown-ass adults where to be, when to be, and how to be.

It's a "have to," not a "get to" or "want to" type decision. And last time I checked, when you treat adults like children, they tend to act like, well, children.

When first stepping into a company as an advisor and consultant, I spend about 85% of my time having conversations about power. Who has it? Who doesn't have it? Who wants it? Who needs it? How does the power structure operate here?

One of my favorite questions to ask is, What's the one thing that everyone knows is true but isn't willing to admit or talk about?

Transaction of power underpins almost everything about the workplace – it feels ubiquitous. There is a deeply held assumption that power is a scarce commodity, that there is not enough to go around. The root of everything that holds organizations back from their full potential has to do with the transaction of power.

We have become familiar with a power structure that looks something like a triangle. At the very top is the leader. Just below are the vice presidents and the trusted advisors. Below them are the managers. Most of the staff are at the bottom of the pyramid – those actually getting the work done. We are proud to have evolved politically out of feudalism and into democracy, but we have not yet done so in the business world.

Power transitions within organizations usually involve replacing one monarch – like the CEO at the top of the pyramid – with another. One older guy is going to retire, and here comes the next. There is another kind of transition of power emerging now: instead of replacing one leader at the top of the pyramid with another, we replace the pyramid itself with something more like a network of nodes, as shown in Figure 3.1.

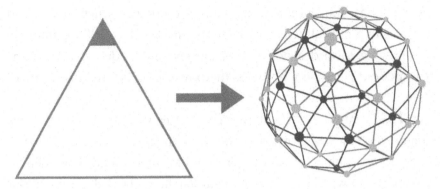

Figure 3.1 Network of nodes

Creating an organizational structure in this way allows for inspiration, energy, and leadership to emerge at any time from anywhere within the system.

In *Reinventing Organizations*, Frederic Laloux explores groundbreaking organizational models that challenge the traditional, hierarchical approach to power and leadership.[2] He introduces the concept of *teal organizations*, which embody a level of consciousness that prioritizes the collective well-being and the pursuit of a shared purpose over individual ego or profit motives.

Teal organizations operate on self-management principles, decentralizing power in a way that enables a more organic and fluid distribution of leadership and decision-making.

Laloux makes the case that traditional top-down power dynamics, often characterized by rigid control and a lack of flexibility, are becoming obsolete in a world that demands rapid adaptation and innovation. The shift from power at the top to being distributed through the network creates a more resilient and responsive structure where diverse perspectives can be heard, leading to better and more innovative solutions.

Making a transition to a network-based power structure is a bold move and a radical departure from the monarch-like CEO paradigm. By moving toward a network of empowered nodes, organizations can not only change who holds the power but also are able to redefine what power means.

The Occupy movement emerged in this way, as did Black Lives Matter, the #MeToo movement, and even the internet itself – a shared meme (the original definition being an idea that spreads from person to person) in which people could participate and collaborate without any single leader calling the shots from the top.

In *New Power*, Jeremy Heimans and Henry Timms, contrasts "new power" with "old power."[3] New power is characterized by participatory engagement and peer-driven decision-making. No longer held by a few at the top, power is instead distributed among networks of people who are united by a cause or a platform. New power challenges traditional notions of hierarchy and authority, proposing that the most impactful and lasting changes often arise from decentralized, collective action.

The Role of Perception in Power Dynamics

One of the best authors on power is Robert Greene. He's written seven international bestselling books on strategy and power. In the corporate arena, his principles suggest power isn't about overt displays of authority; it's about subtle and strategic influence. There's an art to maintaining control by being deliberate and calculated in actions, rather than impulsive. Our true influence often lies in our ability to subtly direct outcomes and perceptions to shape an environment in an almost imperceptible way.

The perception of power is as critical as the actual possession of it. How others view an individual or a group can significantly dictate their actual influence. This idea plays out in organizational settings where leaders who project confidence and competence, even in uncertain situations, often garner more respect and authority.

Greene's work highlights the importance of managing appearances, suggesting that projecting a certain image can be a powerful tool for gaining and maintaining influence. However, he also cautions against the pitfalls of deception and the eventual repercussions of manipulating perceptions without substance to back it up.

With great respect, I enjoy reading his books, but I don't choose to accept this is *all* humans are capable of. We can do better.

The Language of Power

The workplace is flooded with words and phrases that have the word *power* baked into them.

We aim to make our presentations and reports *powerful*.
Whoever exerts more power is a *powerhouse*.
The ones with less freedom and choices are *powerless*.
One party will *overpower* another in order to assume the top dog position, and whoever wins in this race for power does so through *willpower*.
Someone with extraordinary talents is known to have *superpowers*.

A series of movie franchises in the last many years, most of which have evolved from comic books of the 1950s, tell the tales of superheroes with superpowers, an enactment of the archetype of strength and confidence *mostly* without vulnerability. When this cultural influence enters the workplace, it encourages people to lean into the areas where they feel confident and avoid areas where they could learn or grow.

The Drug of Power

In order to free ourselves from power dynamics, we first need to understand what compels us to play the power game over and over again. There are two windows we can use to understand the compulsion toward playing with power: one is from a psychological developmental perspective and the other is understanding the socio-economic system in which we all play.

From birth, we are conditioned to give up our personal agency and follow rules we do not fully understand by our parents, religion, education system, medical system, politics, and eventually our workplaces.

Dr. Shefali Tsabary, a renowned expert in conscious parenting, writes about how many of us were raised in an authoritarian style of parenting, where we were expected to follow instructions without question. A typical interaction might go like this:[4]

Parent: Go wash your hands before dinner.

Child: Why?

Parent: Because I said so.

Dr. Shefali advocates for a radical shift from this type of parenting to a conscious one of mutual respect and connection. In her view, parenting shouldn't be about imposing rules from a pedestal of authority, but about guiding and learning alongside our children. A conscious parenting approach might look more like:

Parent: It's important to wash our hands before eating to keep germs away and stay healthy. It's one of the ways we take care of our bodies. Do you remember why it's important to be healthy?

Child: So we can play and not get sick?

Parent: Exactly! And when we're healthy, we feel good and can have more fun. Let's go wash our hands together.

This approach turns a simple directive into a moment of learning and connection. It's not just about the act of washing hands; it's about instilling an understanding of health, self-care, and personal responsibility. Dr. Shefali's perspective is that every interaction is an opportunity to empower our children, helping them understand the why behind actions, nurturing their curiosity, and respecting their emerging individuality. By moving away from the "because I said so" mentality, we open a dialogue that respects the child's intelligence and fosters a sense of cooperation and understanding rather than compliance and obedience.

In school, many of us were taught to recite facts by heart, most of which were not immediately relevant to our needs or interests. The entire school system with standardized tests and hours sitting in rows of desks was designed to create workers who take direction, not critical thinkers and creators. We weren't meant to be cogs in machines, which is why many of us grow up unhappy and rebelling against the system.

A great majority of conditioning we experienced as children was oriented toward not being curious and not understanding why things are the way they are. We're taught to blindly accept "this is just how it is" and not ask questions. This creates an ingrained habit of obedience, which is perfect for workplaces organizing people within a larger social structure.

If you want to prepare people to wake up early in the morning, put on uncomfortable clothes, travel on crowded freeways, sit in back-numbing chairs, under blinding overhead lights, performing meaningless tasks, in depersonalized environments, you need to train them from an early age to comply with rules they don't understand.

Because of this conditioning, we've become prey to advertising campaigns, political manipulation, celebrity worship, and conformity to idealized stereotypes on social media. We've been systematically robbed of the most important thing we need to enjoy life: a sense of true meaning and purpose. And that's a huge price to pay.

The Power of No

If you're a parent, you know about the "terrible twos." That's when kids first learn their own sovereignty and take a step into their personal power by learning to say the word *no*. Sadly though, no is not allowed in most families and organized societies. It's frowned on to say no, particularly when children do it.

This is the beginning of our experience with power dynamics. Experimenting with the word *no* teaches us to set boundaries and make real choices in our lives. But instead of experiencing the empowerment of real choice, we experience the dynamic of power over, and we grow accustomed to, and accepting of, hierarchy and our place in it.

If you are not getting fed the real food of love and appreciation, then playing with power becomes the only way to make space for yourself and have an impact. As a result, if all of your efforts are squashed, you will either become passive to life or learn to imitate power over others from your parents and teachers.

In elementary and middle school, everyone sort of plays in the same sandbox. Once we get to high school, people splinter into different archetypes, which often sets up relationships to power that last entire lifetimes. There's the athletic jock, who's usually very popular, the academic who crushes all the tests, the indie rebel, the cheerleader, and the preppy kid with a nice sports car, whose parents are extraordinarily wealthy.

Some kids emerge as brokers of power and others tend to follow the rules, and some question the whole game. You can already anticipate – before anyone gets a paying job – who will wield power, who will gladly submit, and who will ask disruptive questions. People find their own place in the system and at work, relative to the identity they developed in high school.

Organizational direction is often determined by decisions made by the CEO or founder, like Steve Jobs, Jeff Bezos, or Bill Gates – geniuses with thousands of helpers. One person at the top will gather close collaborators around them, where almost all the important decisions are made, and then pass directives down through the hierarchy to be implemented.

In many technology companies, careful to protect their intellectual property, decisions are made in secret in a boardroom so people working in design, assembly, or sales might not be in the know of things planned, which affects their ability to plan and execute.

If everything originates from the top, who is going to ask the disruptive questions that organizations need to evolve and grow? It's certainly not going to be those at the top, addicted to having power over others. The cogs, those conditioned to carry out orders, aren't going to ask disruptive questions either because their interest is in gaining approval and ensuring security.

It is probably the indie misfit, who was writing poetry and playing guitar in high school, who was predisposed to questioning the system. Generally, people with those kinds of strengths end up being professors, writers, artists, or musicians, not in our companies helping disrupt the status quo.

Addiction to Power

Typically, there are two types of people relative to power: those who wield it and those who yield it, willingly give it away.

Psychologist Doug Brackman, author of *Driven*, suggested about 2% to 3% of the population can be clinically defined as

71

psychopaths – people who have abnormally low empathy and are willing to cause harm to others in order to fulfill their own agenda (often involving power). Brackman suggested this small percentage of the population is not necessarily maleficent by choice; they are just hardwired toward an addiction to power.[5]

People who crave power often design hierarchical structures in their favor, in which others find their place. Those who are more obedient fit into that structure and climb the corporate ladder as they've been told to do, even if they don't have a strong internal motivation to do so. The striving to ascend a hierarchical system can happen out of a real craving for power or out of obedience and in turn, keeps the cog going to reinforce the system for those most in power.

At one time, this was a monarchy: a king with absolute power and subjects in a descending hierarchy of agency all the way down to serfs. This became somewhat decentralized with feudalism: the dominance of a wealthy landowner and workers who were protected by a benevolent overlord or abused by a malevolent one.

At SHIFT, we have seen a recurring theme emerge for the people we work with. Many begin their careers fueled by a vision to make a meaningful impact on the world. As time passes, they find themselves deeply entrenched in the relentless pursuit of corporate success. This journey, often spanning decades, sometimes leads to a startling realization: the ladder of success they've been climbing is not propped against the wall of their true aspirations.

So how can we move beyond the conventional definitions of success to embrace a life of deeper fulfillment and purpose? Although I don't pretend to know all the answers, I do know seeking a path that aligns closely with your inner values and desires is a good start. And instead of pursuing achievement, focus on what truly brings joy and fulfillment.

For many, especially those leaving the corporate world, the shift in focus is liberating. It marks a departure from pursuing success as defined by society toward self-actualization and meaningful engagement. In this light, our lives are measured by growth, contribution, and impact over titles and accolades.

And although this sounds like a worthy pursuit, it's difficult for many because of the conditioning that achievement is the holy grail and our value as a human is measured by how much money we make, how many degrees we've collected, and sometimes how many followers we have on social media.

Climbing the Ladder

Once the context has been created by those who crave power, the entire game becomes about fear and power. Without some people living in fear, others cannot wield power. After several decades of working in organizational development, I've recognized almost all organizations are framed within this unquestioned assumption of hierarchy and the expectation to desire ascending to the top of the power structure.

We're in a time where for a number of reasons, we are experiencing the decentralization of power, both in the way we inhabit existing structures and the ways we create new ones. For the first time, we are experiencing five generations working together in the workforce. Younger people are often more educated and smarter than they were in the past. Established norms are getting disrupted as we find new and better ways to do things. And in the business world, relative to organizational structure, we still very much have a centralization of power that people are willing to do anything to take control of.

We Are All Affected

When we recognize situations involve an imbalance of power, we tend to want to blame the one wielding the power, but we often fail to see that everyone in the system participates.

Because of the way we're raised and conditioned to submit to authority, we are taught not to create but to memorize and regurgitate. The training ground of obedience up to the age of seven reinforces neural pathways in the brain that make conformity natural and familiar, slowly shutting down the parts of the brain required to think outside the box. We become resigned to subjugation.

In his book *Driven*, Doug Brackman attributes some of this to changes that happened in our neurology after the agricultural revolution. Previously, most homo sapiens were hunters. The neurology and brain activity were designed for risk, new and unprecedented situations, and thinking quickly outside the box. With the advent of farming, a completely different kind of neural pattern was required, and, according to Brackman, it affected as much as 90% of the population.[6]

For a farmer to get good crops, they need to be able to remember what they did last year, modify it, tweak it slightly, and then repeat it. It's dangerous to change things too radically because if they don't work out, they might not survive the next winter.

Farmer neurology, as Brackman calls it, does not encourage innovation because there's no motive. According to Brackman, somewhere about 10% of the population have pure, undiluted, farmer-type genes. They require clear and unambiguous instructions that they can follow. Faced with an unprecedented emergency, such a person would not know what to do.

Brackman also suggests about 10% of the population have pure hunter genes, attuned to novelty and abstract thinking. They usually become disruptive entrepreneurs and are designed to work in unpredictable environments.

And then there's the middle 80% who have some mixture of these two genetic dispositions. When encouraged by their environment to be curious and think on their feet, their hunter genetics will be activated. If they're too conditioned toward obedience, these hunter instincts will be shut down and they will comply.

Never Underestimate the Comfort of a Pattern

Changing a pattern is uncomfortable. Our fear of the unknown is often greater than the pain of the known, which paralyzes us to stay where we are, doing what we're doing, even though it's no longer serving us. We settle for "good enough," because that is less daunting than venturing into the wild unknown.

And what constitutes a position "good enough" to never leave? Good enough doesn't mean you're satisfied with your job, lit up by the values of the organization you work for, or fired up by the impact you're having. It's good enough because it takes less effort and energy to do what you're doing than doing something different. Even when it feels like an unrelenting, miserable grind.

If you put dogs in a cage with an electrocuted floor but give them a little platform to hop up onto, as soon as they figure out the environment, they will move to the platform and avoid the floor. However, if you put the dogs in a cage where both the floor and the platform give them shocks so that they get no respite, there is nowhere for them to go.

Should this inescapable condition persist, and eventually a safe platform is introduced, the dogs, interestingly, fail to use it. Over time, they adopt a resigned mindset, succumbing to the belief that avoiding the shocks is futile.

This phenomenon is rooted in the concept of learned helplessness, a theory put forward by psychologists Martin Seligman and Steven Maier in 1967 based on observations from their canine experiments.[7] Initially subjected to inescapable electric shocks, the dogs learned to believe that their situation was hopeless and that their actions had no effect on their outcomes.

Consequently, even when given the opportunity to evade the shocks later on, they didn't take action. This concept of learned helplessness has been instrumental in understanding certain human psychological states, illustrating how exposure to uncontrollable adverse events can lead to a state of passivity and resignation, profoundly affecting behavior and perceptions of control.

It is simply not worth the energy to explore something different. The same thing happens when you keep an eagle in a cage long enough. When you finally open the cage to free it, the eagle will not move because imprisonment has become its normal state.

Outsourcing Meaning

Once we have been trained in this kind of learned helplessness, disconnected from our capacity to think for ourselves, we repeat this in every part of our lives. We look to motivational speakers and self-help gurus to improve our well-being and direction in life. We simply pray our politicians will determine a sustainable future for our children. We outsource happiness and self-worth for others to fulfill. As long as we keep up these habitual patterns, we are unlikely to have a purpose-filled work experience.

Even today, after $1.4 trillion has been pumped into team building, consulting, and organizational development, many people will say, "I have a job," or "I'm looking for a job," instead of "I'm looking for an opportunity to fully express my gifts and allow my talents to shine."[8]

In our work within organizations, generational differences can be stark relative to how people experience and what they expect from work. Boomers and Generation Xers seem to be more oriented to longevity and less likely to take risks whereas millennials and possibly Gen Z (although it's still too early to conclude) seem to be more inclined to expect to do work that is stimulating, enjoyable, and aligned with their purpose of making a real contribution to the world.

Trust Your Gut

Researchers like Daniel Goleman tell us that people who move through unpredictable situations really well make decisions not from a cognitive process in the prefrontal cortex but from a sense of *knowing,* which comes from the gut.[9] Many of us have been trained not to trust our intuition but assume other people know better, so by the time we become adults, we have no confidence left in what feels right or wrong.

We turn to somebody who appears confident about what to do. The abbreviation for a man who exudes habitual confidence is a *con man.*

In experimenting with emerging ways of running organizations, we have learned that when you invite people from all parts of the organization to be in dialogue, there is actually not one singular, correct narrative but multiple narratives that may seem contradictory to logic but actually allow for more complex and sophisticated thinking.

When we shift an organization from a pyramid to a network of interconnected nodes, we discover everyone within the organization has a piece of the mosaic and guiding vision, and practical solutions emerge that would have been unavailable to any individual acting alone.

Everyone Loses

Within any social system or organization that involves an imbalance of power, we are tempted to assume the serfs at the bottom of the feudal system lose out and the monarchs or CEOs are the winners. From the lens of financial metrics, this is a fair conclusion to make.

77

When Jeff Bezos is worth hundreds of billions of dollars and people packing boxes at Amazon are making minimum wage, carrying debt, and struggling to afford their groceries, it clearly looks like there are winners and losers in the game. When we look at other metrics, it is not so black and white.

During the 1930s and World War II, it certainly looked like the members of the Nazi Party were the winners: they got to own valuable art, eat at the finest restaurants, and live in mansions previously owned by those they dominated. But ask anyone in Germany whose parents were involved in the Nazi movement, and you will hear a different story. The people who appeared to be winners paid a huge price, one that was frequently passed on to their descendants for several generations. They lost their humanity, heart, innocence, and capacity for intimacy.

Historians tell us a similar account of those who got wealthy during the Industrial Revolution. Certain families made more money and had more material security, but there was always a price – increased likelihood of alcoholism, estrangement within families, and even suicide, which was often passed down through later generations.

When we work within organizations, we seek to talk to as many stakeholders as possible, not just those who spend time in the boardroom. Certainly, those with executive positions earn more money and have greater privileges, but there is also a price to be paid for life at the top.

Martin Seligman and his team at the Center for Positive Psychology at the University of Pennsylvania have measured well-being along 22 metrics.[10] They have determined those with more income, assets, and power are frequently more subject to drug addiction, divorce, estrangement among relatives, and stress-related conditions.

Whether we talk to founders, people on the shop floor, members of the sales team, or middle management, we hear the same narrative. Everyone tells us they don't feel their time is their own. They don't feel empowered to organize themselves at work – rather, they're being organized, or controlled. And surprisingly, many CEOs also feel this way because they are also carrying out instructions whether it be from their board or pandering to the demands of their clients and employees.

If both those at the apex and the base of the pyramid feel equally disenfranchised, who then is doing the controlling?

There Is No They

There seems to be this super identity, this invisible hand, the all-knowing controller of the world we refer to as *they*. At times we put great faith in they and say things like, "Sooner or later, they will discover a cure for cancer" or "They will solve global climate change." Equally, we attribute all the world's worst evils to *they*. "They are destroying the environment." "They treat us like cogs in the machine." Whenever I hear *they*, I always think, "Have you ever met this entity referred to as *they?*"

Part of the reclaiming of personal sovereignty, which we will address in Chapter 4, is to abandon the notion of *they* altogether and realize there is only *we*. We need to fix the problems by turning inward and first taking a good hard look at ourselves, and then working together to change the bad thinking, behaviors, patterns, and systems that got us here.

For example, why doesn't Harvard allocate $40 billion from its endowment to offer education to the entire population? Imagine the possibility of everyone accessing a few online courses from one of the best universities on the planet. Virtual learning, after all, incurs marginal costs and essentially requires only a username and password. However, such a move could dilute its exclusivity, potentially alienate its donors, and diminish its own status and influence – and ultimately power.

Ultimately, the power imbalances at play right now in the world are completely unsustainable. Not only the financial equity gap but also the equity gap in creativity, decision-making, and innovation. Before we change the world and the organizations we work in, we must turn inward first.

After 20+ years of consulting with organizations all over the world, we discovered that before we can make any meaningful changes within an organization, we must encourage people to think about what they personally value the most. Of course, the surface-level answers are about the amount of money they make, if they get to work remotely, and if they have a visible path to the top.

And when we go deeper, that's where the magic happens. We ask questions like "What brings you the most joy?" "What keeps you up at night?" "What gets you up in the morning?"

We talk about loneliness, the meaning of human connection, enthusiasm and dread, resilience and fear. When we do this, we watch organizations and people shift from a place that manufactures widgets by cogs to one where people can express themselves fully and unapologetically.

These kinds of questions bring into focus the reality that many other kinds of equity are being spent and gained within organizations outside of the conventional metrics of money and prestige.

What Say You?

Part 1: Understanding our relationship with power and how we hold power ourselves can be helpful as we navigate our daily lives with work and in relationships with others. Here are a few questions to ask yourself. And, quick pro tip: if you're going to take the time to do the exercise, be fully, unapologetically honest because *only* from that place can you create change.

1. What is your relationship to power? Are you more of a power wielder or do you give your power away? (Initial inkling is probably spot on!)

2. Think back to your childhood, what were you taught about saying no, asking questions, or pushing back on power?

3. How did you respond and where does that type of response show up today in the face of power?

4. What were some of your life-changing moments when you decided to do it your way? Recall these memories as vividly as you can: who was there, where you were, what was said, and so on.

5. How did your conditioning affect the way you wield, yield, or hold power now?

Part 2: Finding a life of purpose and fulfillment is easier said than done. Start with these questions; you might find some golden nuggets of insight that will help you find more purpose where you are or pursue another path better for what you're here on earth to do.

1. On a scale of 1 to 10, how much do you truly enjoy your life now?

2. What would need to be true for you to rate it a 10?

3. What are you doing, working on, thinking about when you experience the following:

   - **Selflessness:** where your actions are for others
   - **Timelessness:** when you don't have a sense of time

- **Effortlessness:** when things aren't a struggle, it's happening naturally

4. When do you feel most at peace?

5. When you're not at peace, what is happening? What are the thoughts you're having? Are any of the thoughts rooted in fear? Fear of not being loved, fear of not being enough, fear of not living up to your fullest potential?

Chapter 4

Sovereignty Everywhere

"You have your way. I have my way. As for the right way, the correct way, and the only way, it does not exist."

— Friedrich Nietzsche

Part 1: Impossible Decisions

Once I got into Hopkins, I knew everything was on the line. Life had given me a lucky break, every moment counted, and I'd better not blow it. I spent my three years in college running small businesses, so I was able to make money while getting a diploma. I started a contracting company in my sophomore year that grew to 150 employees by the time I graduated, as well as a couple other entrepreneurial ventures focused on the art of being a better human in business.

I was able to get my mom a place in an assisted living facility so she could live as much of a life as one can, being blind and in a wheelchair with failing kidneys and pancreas.

Just after I graduated, my contracting business went belly-up (a story I wrote about in my first book, *Grow Regardless*). I was in debt and living on fumes. Then, one weekend, I was offered a speaking opportunity for a company that had a program to help high school kids of first-generation immigrants get into college. In a way, I was the epitome of what this program was about: it's not where you start; it's where you end up. It felt like my lucky break.

Before leaving Baltimore to give the talk in Queens, New York, my mom went back in the hospital after having a heart attack. I went to the hospital to speak to my mom's doctor, as I had 100 times before.

"How is she? I asked. "What's going on? How long is she going to be here?"

These are questions I had asked every doctor I spoke to throughout my childhood 1,000 times. My mom got diabetes shortly after having me 23 years earlier and struggled with the disease her whole life. I got the gift of being her caretaker.

"She's going to be here for a very long time," he replied.

"Okay," I said, "I'm going to be gone for three or four days for a quick business trip. Please call me if anything comes up."

"Mom, I'll see you when I get back. Love you. Everything's gonna be fine."

"Joey, I love you, too. And I really want to get out of here," she whispered conspiratorially. She used to jailbreak quite a bit.

"Please don't do that," I replied. "I'll be back after the weekend, in three days."

Fast forward . . .

Just as I am about to go on stage, the guy in charge caught my arm.

"We're putting a lot of faith in you, Joe. You know, we're taking a big chance on you. You started all these companies while still in college. You can give these people hope."

"I promise you," I reassured him. "I won't let you or them down. You know, frankly, I need this break right now."

"This could catapult you into a really successful series of opportunities," he replied. "But if it fails, I don't think you're getting a second chance."

I stepped up onto the stage feeling nervous but pumped up and ready to roll.

"You may be wondering why a 23-year-old kid is standing in front of you today," I begin. "For many of you, I'm probably less than half your age. I have learned from failure how to bounce back, simply because I had to . . ."

I started to tell them the stories of all my successes and failures.

"Sometimes it feels like you're walking through a thick fog, and you've got a flashlight that will illuminate just five feet ahead. You may not see the whole picture. But you know, I got a message from my father that has always felt right to me, to put your best foot forward . . ."

At this point in the talk, my cell phone rang.

Now remember, back then in the early 2000s, hardly anyone had a cell phone. I used it to run my businesses. I looked down and saw the number: my mom's landline at home. She somehow left the hospital facility and went back to her assisted living apartment. I had been through this (drama) so many times. This time, in front of all these people, I felt determined to ignore it. I had developed a multiplicity of awareness.

"I had a mentor . . ." I go on talking to the audience, "who used to be the president of a big bank. I was painting his house . . ."

"I can't believe she's home. I can't believe we're doing this again . . ." said a voice in my head.

"And my mentor, he said to me . . ."

"She's supposed to be in the hospital. But here's a f**king call coming in from her home number . . . I wish she wouldn't make this harder than it needs to be."

I realized I must seem distracted. Some members of the audience are frowning, looking concerned.

"Sorry. He said to me . . . ummm . . . he asked a lot of good questions. He asked me once 'Are you going to conform?'"

"Something is wrong though. Something terrible might happen. She's supposed to be in the hospital. The doctor said she'd be there for months. She should not be calling from home. Something's gone way off track . . ."

"Sorry . . . where was I? 'Are you going to conform or are you going to rise up and do your own thing that makes sense to you?'" The phone is still ringing.

"Excuse me," I finally said to the audience. "I think I've got to take this call." I turned my back on the audience and ran offstage as I answered the call.

She was screaming. "Joey, I need you. I need you . . ."

"Mom," I cut her off, trying my best to speak quietly. "What's going on? Why are you home?"

"I'm looking for my insulin. Where's my insulin?"

"Mom, it's in the fridge," I whispered. "But what are you doing home?"

"I wanted out of the hospital. I want you to come home, Joey."

"Mom, you're not well. Can I just have them come back and get you?"

"I don't want to be there anymore."

"Mom, I can't do this right now. I'm giving a talk. I'm in the middle of something."

"But I need you to be here."

"I can't be there right now."

"I need you here right now. Now." She is shouting. "You've got to come right now."

"Mom, I can't do it. I can't do it this time."

I snapped the phone shut. I felt completely wrenched apart. This was the first time I said no. I turned back to the audience, cleared my throat, and did my best to carry on with the talk.

"So sorry. Where was I? Ah yes, my mentor, he taught me to conform. I mean to not conform. He asked what I really wanted to do. To create. And your children can do the same . . ."

But I had lost the momentum, and my mind was somewhere else; the talk became almost mechanical.

I felt heavy, exhausted, out of enthusiasm, and no ground underneath me.

As I gave the rest of the talk, I felt empty, like a fraud, like I just committed the worst crime imaginable. I felt like a terrible person. And I still had three more talks to do on Sunday.

"What have you done?" The voice in my head returned.

Sovereignty Everywhere

"If you go home right now, you could help your mother. You always answer the call. Like she has always helped you. Maybe something is really off . . ."

"And destroy your career and this opportunity," a contrary voice said. *"You have to make money. This is how you can really care for her. And you can't make yourself your mother's permanent caregiver and never have a life of your own. You have done everything you can to help. You can't always be that person. There has to be a point when you just say no, put up a boundary."*

I got back to Baltimore early Monday morning. I drove past her house twice in my Jeep, but I couldn't bring myself to go in. I drove straight to my father's house, about 25 minutes away, to get my checkbook so I could write a check for her rent and take care of her bills.

When I got to my father's house, his landline phone rang as I walked in the door. I had no idea who it was, but for some random reason, I decided to pick it up.

"This is the Baltimore City Police Department," the voice on the other end of the phone said. "We're looking for Joseph Mechlinski." Instinctively, I knew what was coming next.

"This is he," I gulped.

"I'm so sorry. We've just found your mother dead in her apartment. We'd like you to come over."

Just for a moment, I felt a complete chill of coldness over my body – and a feeling of relief.

Finally, it had arrived, the moment I'd been preparing myself for my whole life. I had played this moment out for decades. My mom was in the hospital multiple times a year. She even survived two pancreas and kidney transplants while I was in college. Dozens of surgeries. Life was hard for her, but she was hard right back.

I took a really deep breath and felt a kind of peace come over me. But then, almost immediately after, my palms got clammy. I was in a cold sweat. I was flooded with guilt and shame. I felt incredibly empty. I understood this would be the saddest moment of my whole life. My whole body was flushed with waves of hurt and pain and a deep heaviness in my eyes.

I punched the wall with full force and came down into a fetal position on the floor. But only for a minute or two. The pain pulling me into myself felt like a black hole with no bottom, and I was afraid if I lingered there for more than a few moments, I would never come out again. This was the 23rd person close to me who had died, and I was 23 years old.

Mechanically, I drove over to her place. I called my father on the way, and he met me there.

Her body was still in the bathroom where they had found her. She was sprawled out on the floor, blood splattered on the wall, and a smell of death in the room. The whole atmosphere had a heavy density. I couldn't feel anything; it was like I was staring at a movie about someone else's life.

As though voices were coming from the end of a long tunnel, I heard them telling me they estimated she had been dead for at least a day. The body was beginning to smell.

In situations like this, you expect some drama: flashing lights and cops everywhere, like in the movies. But in real life, it was all quite dull. There was just the front desk clerk from the assisted living facility and one police officer who seemed almost bored. The coroner arrived with a body bag, and I helped them wheel her out and put her in the back of a car.

I walked back to my Jeep with my father.

"She's finally at peace," he said. "Joey, no one could have done more than you did for her. You were there for her your whole life."

"Dad, she called me on Saturday. She was begging for help. If I'd gone back then, I could have saved her."

"Joey," my father laid his hand gently on my shoulder. "You couldn't be in that role forever. You've done so much already.

At some point, you just had to live. You made the best decisions available to you, given impossible choices."

One of the big unanswered questions, which I think we all grapple with is, "Why me?"

Why did I get born with this diabetic underage mother?

Why was I born into all this stuff to deal with?

Why couldn't I just have some kind of a stable deal?

Why couldn't I just get a break?

I realize, years later, if I had not passed through the excruciating pain of all these pivotal moments, I would not be who I am today.

Although that moment with my mother was agonizing and dramatic, I understand now that we are all constantly faced with impossible choices, where it seems like there's no security no matter what choice you make.

It's our opportunity to go from passenger to co-pilot.

Part 2: Personal Sovereignty

In previous chapters, I've talked about the imbalance of power and how pervasive this is, particularly in the world of business. Once we recognize these power plays, and we discover the part of ourselves that is committed to stepping out of those games, it leads to legitimate and fascinating questions.

- What would life look like if you stepped out of participating in power dynamics?

- What would it look like if you gave up your need to exert power over someone else or relinquish your power to someone else?

- Within the constraints of our socioeconomic system, inherited wealth, and inequities of opportunity and education among certain groups, is it even possible?

Let's explore.

The phrase people commonly use for living a life free of power hierarchies is *personal sovereignty*. Sometimes it's something we have to experience to fully understand, more than we can define intellectually.

Personal sovereignty means to live life as if it's a movie in which you are the main actor, the director, and the screenwriter. This movie is not so much about you getting ahead of other people or being successful relative to others' failure, but more about your development and full actualization as a whole human being.

The practice of personal sovereignty means you don't become second fiddle to anyone else, nor do you allow anyone to become second fiddle to you. This can be quite a challenge because we are so habituated to imbalanced relationships, not only as they play out through personal codependency but also in education, religion, spirituality, politics, and work.

Let's get real: very few people live with a significant degree of personal sovereignty because it requires the hard work of understanding why we have given away sovereignty in the first place and then learning how to regain it. It also means taking a courageous stand, which may need to be asserted again and again, day after day, against the norms of mainstream society, particularly in the workplace.

Here's a quick important caveat:

When we say you are the star, director, and screenwriter of the movie of your life in a way that defies logic but works out well in practice, you see that in everyone you meet as well.

Once you have recognized your own personal sovereignty, as soon as you shine the light of your awareness on another person, you see the same is true for others, too: they are the star, director, and screenwriter of the movie of their life.

As we will discover later in this chapter, one of the key symptoms of personal sovereignty, as well as the most effective way to regain it, is deeply tied to deliberate creative acts. Whenever you do something you've been told to do, or because it's just the way it's always been done, you are surrendering your sovereignty and allowing yourself to be overpowered.

Often, the knee jerk instinct to avoid being overpowered is to push back and exert power over others, to play the same game. When you take a creative act, you are not playing with power but asserting sovereignty. You're not playing the game, you're stepping away from the board. You can do that alone or together with other people.

These creative acts are deeply tied to seeing life through the lens of radical acceptance and responsibility, the idea that you are completely in control of your life and your state of being at any and every point in time.

Sometimes people object to this idea because gross economic and political injustices, systemic racism, massive inequality of living standard between different nations, and countless other factors make the practice of radical responsibility an idea only available to the privileged and entitled.

Practicing radical responsibility is not intended to be a truth that negates social inequality but a parallel way of seeing things more connected to how we deal with challenging circumstances, rather than the fact that they obviously exist.

Katie Hendricks, who has spoken and written extensively about personal sovereignty, calls this *authoring yourself*. Authoring yourself is about how you package yourself in the world, listen to and express your own creative juices, and share your purpose with the world.[1]

The practice of personal responsibility generally begins with the kind of disruptive thinking I have invited – questioning every rule we have ever participated within and asking "Who made the rules about what is possible and not possible? Are they actually valid or true and in everyone's well-being?"

The rigorous practice of sovereignty can get us very deep into this process of pruning the garden. Even gravity is up for grabs. What if gravity itself is just a shared agreement? The solidity of objects?

Clearly, a few people have questioned even these very fundamental assumptions about reality, or the word *levitation* would not exist in our lexicon. And the particulate wave-like nature of subatomic particles within quantum physics supports the notion that our belief in the solidity of things may be just that: a self-fulfilling prophecy.

Obviously, this book is not a manual for levitation or passing your hand through a solid wall. These questions reinforce the understanding that the only limits within which we live are the ones we have agreed to believe in. Personal sovereignty requires us to question all that.

Sovereignty Everywhere

Personal sovereignty is something we're all familiar with experientially, but it can be difficult to talk about because it defies so many of our shared assumptions. One of the best ways to see sovereignty come alive is in certain extraordinary movies.

Examples of films that evoke the sense of personal sovereignty are *Slumdog Millionaire*, *Forrest Gump*, and Roberto Benini's *Life Is Beautiful*. In such films, the one who has the power is often the villain and not a sympathetic character. It is the underdog, with relatively little power, equity, or opportunity who is exerting sovereignty – not in winning, but in their relationship to the fluctuations of winning and losing.

Pig is likely the most powerful example of personal sovereignty. Nicolas Cage plays Robin Feld, a former world-renowned chef who decided 15 years previously, at the top of his game, to unplug from the power games inherent in the high-end restaurant business, live in the woods, and play by his own rules. He has a beloved truffle pig and a subsistence living. After his pig is stolen and he is badly beaten, Feld goes on a quest to get his pig back. He shows up at a fancy restaurant that uses truffles in its menu.

The chef, Derek, was once a prep cook for Feld before he fired him. Once they recognize each other, they enter into a tense dialogue where Derek proudly explains his "concept" of serving cutting-edge dishes with local ingredients.

Feld reminds Derek that at one time he had a dream of opening a pub where the signature dish would be liver Scotch eggs with a honey curry mustard.

Derek gets flustered and defensive, now confused about the way he has sold out to play the game. In lines that redefine the film, Feld tells Derek it's all fake, a game, one that Derek is basically playing in service of others. He implores Derek to wake up before there's less of him, before he doesn't recognize himself.

This interaction highlights how much we live our lives for others, whether it's our parents, teachers, boss, spouse, partners, or friends, and how little we live on our own terms.

The Limits of Myopicism

The late Daniel Kahneman won the Nobel Prize in Economic Sciences in 2002 for the work he did with Amos Tversky on the inherent biases in our thinking patterns. He went on to write the seminal book *Thinking Fast and Slow*, in which he names the various irrational shortcuts our brain takes to make sense of things; they create blind spots and can lead us astray.[2] To me, the most interesting of these biases is what he calls the *availability bias*. To put it simply, it means we know things, and then we also know we don't know some things. But there is a much greater number of things we don't even know that we don't know.

This kind of cognitive bias is also sometimes called the *Dunning-Kruger effect*, whereby "people with limited knowledge or competence in a given intellectual or social domain greatly overestimate their knowledge or competence in that domain relative to objective criteria or the performance of their peers, or people in general."[3]

In a nutshell, we all greatly overestimate our abilities.

For example, a recent poll conducted by Hartford Financial Services discovered 88% of poll respondents considered themselves "cautious drivers."[4] Another similar study found 80% of survey respondents rated themselves "above average" to other drivers. Statistically, this is an impossibility. If 80% of a group were "above average," then that average would not be average![5]

This kind of narrow vision, where we overestimate what we think we know and remain unaware of the things we don't know is also sometimes referred to as *myopicism*, which means to be short-sighted.

It also has a secondary meaning: "lacking in foresight or discernment, narrow in perspective and without concern for broader implications."[6] We only see part of the puzzle, but think we see all of it.

In his book *Driven*, the psychologist Doug Brackman emphasizes how much this capacity to overemphasize what we think we know makes us short-sighted. "Humility is simply the capacity to be honest with oneself. It's an absence of pride."[7]

He remembers how one of his professors once told him, "Becoming a PhD is considered to be the way to become an expert in something. But true expertise is realizing how much you don't know about something. We develop pride in the area because it covers the shame we feel for being not enough. We create an artificial persona who acts like an expert."

"There is no way to create a sovereign environment," Brackman said, "until we can fully digest humility. Sovereignty has a direct linear relationship with humility. The more you know you don't know, the more creative you become. We don't need any more experts. A more humble workforce would be phenomenal because when we meet together in *not knowing* and share creativity, we come up with much better solutions."

Deeply understanding the limits created by myopicism gives us a much more nuanced understanding of sovereignty.

We can understand real sovereignty arising through four developmental phases.

In the first phase, we find ourselves trapped in a negative worldview generated by our own pessimistic thoughts. We are full of doubt and cynicism. In that state, when we come across someone who appears to know what they're doing or has an upbeat message, it's easy to say, we recognize our own doubt and cynicism and become open to a better way.

In the second phase, we look for inspiration from the outside, from "thought leaders." This certainly seems like a serious upgrade from the spiral of negative thinking we can get caught up in on our own. But, as unintended collateral damage, we negate our power and outsource our sovereignty and inspiration to other people. This is like singing a cover song – someone else's song and not your own.

In the third phase, we recognize we have given away our sovereignty and outsourced our inspiration to others, and we begin to dig deeper within ourselves to find our own truth and values. *This is what I believe. This is what's true for me. I'm going to act from my own integrity now.* This is a huge step in the direction of personal authority: finding your unique song.

When we dig deep within ourselves in this way, it appears this step should be the end – that we should be connected to inner knowing or a kind of "divine light" from within. Almost always, it proves unrealistic because each and every human being is, to some degree, myopic. Everyone is living within their own private simulation, a personal version of the truth, but not the whole thing.

To experience the fourth phase, remember the story of the elephant who wanders into a village of blind people. Someone touches the tail and says, "Oh, simple. The elephant's like a rope." Someone else touches one of the elephant's legs and says, "No, no, this elephant is like a tree with a big trunk." Someone else touches the elephant's snout and says, "You're all wrong. The elephant is like a big hose." Nobody is wrong about the nature of the elephant. Each person is seeing part of the story.

If these blind villagers could compare notes and trust each other's experience as much as their own, they would be able to share their pieces of the jigsaw puzzle and come up with a bigger truth. There are two ways to get beyond this into the fourth phase of sovereignty. One is collaboration with others and the other is to find ways to transcend the localized perspective through mystical experience.

Cultural Flywheel: Fostering a Community of Cocreation

Cocreation unfolds as a symphony of humility and collaboration, grounded in the understanding that wisdom doesn't reside in a single individual but is dispersed among many. This ethos compels us to not only seek input from others but also to deeply value the diversity of thought they bring to the table.

Drawing inspiration from anthropological insights, there's a sweet spot for fostering such collaboration – often cited as about 150 members (thanks to Robert Dunbar, an anthropologist and evolutionary psychologist)). This "magic number" enables an organization to harness a broad spectrum of viewpoints while ensuring each connection remains meaningful. This balance is crucial for nurturing an environment where innovative ideas can flourish and every voice can be heard.

Redefining leadership within this context moves beyond traditional hierarchies to emphasize a model of "cocreating coordinated movement." This approach is pivotal in realizing a shared vision, wherein leadership transforms into a practice of harmonizing diverse contributions to achieve a collective goal.

Central to this philosophy is the eradication of power imbalances, which hinder the free exchange of ideas and stifle the creative process. In contrast to the zero-sum game of traditional power dynamics, cocreation champions a generative approach where the whole becomes greater than the sum of its parts.

An example of this oneness is found in flocks of birds called starlings. There is no leader, but they create patterns and shapes of the flock that look like near magic, always staying in formation together.

To ensure the vitality of this cocreation culture, a feedback flywheel mechanism is instrumental (see Figure 4.1). This model goes beyond linear feedback systems, integrating a cyclical process that

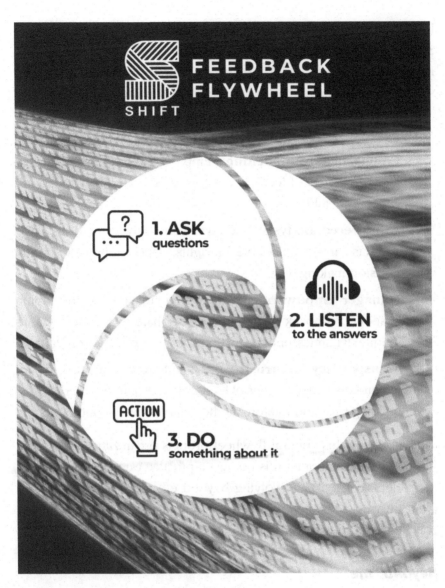

Figure 4.1 The feedback flywheel

leverages employee insights, data analytics, and sentiment analysis. Such a comprehensive feedback loop is essential for continuous improvement and for cultivating an environment where diverse perspectives are not just included but integral to the organizational fabric.

Actionable Steps to Activate the Cultural Flywheel

- **Comprehensive listening:** Employ a broad approach to gather a variety of feedback, recognizing both direct communication and subtle cues.

- **AI-powered analysis:** Use advanced analytics to distill large datasets into actionable insights, accelerating informed decision-making.

- **Manager empowerment:** Support managers in developing bespoke feedback systems that resonate with their team's unique dynamics, enhancing both autonomy and accountability.

- **Transparency and trust:** Foster a culture of openness, where the process and outcomes of feedback are communicated clearly, building trust and reinforcing the value of every contribution.

Embracing this cultural flywheel propels organizations toward a future where collaboration is not just a practice but a cornerstone of their identity. It's about evolving beyond efficient processes to create a thriving ecosystem where every participant is engaged in the cocreation journey toward excellence.

Beyond "Me"

Exploring the depths of how we perceive individuality within an organization offers a unique pathway to transcend narrow-mindedness. This journey into understanding the self asks us to reconsider what it means to be a sovereign entity. Is there truly a separate being, or is this notion an illusion?

Philosopher and writer Ken Wilber's concept of "holons" provides a fascinating lens through which to view this question. Each human being, or holon, is not merely an isolated entity but a part of a greater whole – a whole-on, embodying both wholeness and a part of a larger system.[8]

Our physical form, distinct as it may seem, is in essence a manifestation of the earth itself. Every cell within us is nourished and replenished by the earth's bounty, making our bodies animated expressions of the Greek goddess and personification of earth, Gaia. Moreover, the myriad thoughts and emotions that flow through us, though perceived as personal, are largely influenced by the collective consciousness. They are shared, rather than unique to the individual.

Beyond the physical and the mental lies another dimension – often referred to as the spirit. This aspect, elusive and intangible, both animates and witnesses our existence. It's in this realm that the concept of individual sovereignty begins to blur. As we delve deeper into our core, seeking our true values, we encounter a profound connection to something far greater than ourselves.

This exploration uncovers not just personal values but also universal ones, bridging the gap between the individual and the collective. Through Wilber's perspective, agency emerges not from asserting our separateness but from recognizing and embracing our interconnectedness with the universe. It suggests that transcending our perceived individuality enables us to tap into a broader, more inclusive understanding of existence and our place within it.

Become an Agent

If I were to tell you my friend Ava is an agent, what would you think? You might imagine she's a real estate agent, a literary agent, or a manager. Whichever kind of agent she is, it means she is a representative of another party. She's in the middle, negotiating between something or someone that has a great deal to offer and their potential audience.

A literary agent does not take personal credit for the work they represent; they would not say, "I wrote this book," but "I represent the one who wrote the book, and I want to help its wisdom reach more people." All the deference and praise is given to the original author. A good agent is someone who defers everything to the real source of brilliance.

True agency means there is no sense of things coming from you; they come through you from another source. Show up and get out of the way.

As well as cocreation and collaboration, this sense of agency can be an important element of true sovereignty – a sense of something bigger than yourself moving through you and aligning with that force. It means your work becomes a calling to be of service to something beyond yourself, rather than a way to get money or personal fame.

The more we see work as a calling rather than a job you do to pay for the rest of your life, the more the barriers break down between life at home and life at work. Every moment is part of being an agent for something beyond yourself, and you become a whole person, showing up with all of you to every part of your life.

Bringing All of You to Work

The notion of bringing your whole self to work is relatively new. Even 20 or 30 years ago, you would most often hear people say, "You've got to leave your personal life at home. Leave everything at the front door as you walk into the office," or people would say, "This is about business. It's not personal."

But as we saw with the Great Resignation, people started to wake up and honor more of their full selves. This accentuated what was already happening with the increase of women in the workplace in the since the 1950s.

Prior, women were often encouraged not to work, relegated to "feminine" type of roles, or simply not hired due to the traditional expectation that women are here to be wives, mothers, and home-makers. In fact, a single mom today probably gets more done in an hour than a corporate executive gets done in a whole day.

My wife, Erica, launched a podcast called *Working Mom Hour* with this exact notion in mind, with the mission of building a community of moms who are bringing the immense skill set they have developed at home into the way they work.

There are huge advantages to bringing all of yourself to work and abandoning this segregation of personal and professional. But arguably the most important gain is the chance to feel more psychologically safe in the workplace.

I mentioned Google published the Project Aristotle Study in the Introduction to this book.[9] They wanted to better understand the factors driving higher performance in some of their teams over others. After studying hundreds of teams and tens of thousands of workers, they were able to identify one common core component shared by the great majority of high performers, which they termed *psychological safety*.

This defined the culture of teams who could create environments where everyone felt seen, safe, and supported – feeling like the organization has your back. It means each member of the team knows they will not be judged and others will accept them exactly as they are, including their shadow, their quirks, and all the things that make us human.

This kind of psychological safety means you're not withholding, suppressing, or scared of being found out or failing. One of the main advantages to psychological safety is the freedom to try something different and take risks.

This all began to change on March 16, 2020, when the world began to realize we no longer have to be chained to a desk to get work done. As business meetings shifted from the boardroom to Zoom calls, your coworkers could see your kitchen, your artwork, your dog, and even your children.

This increased relaxation enabled people to show up to meetings wearing just the same things they would wear on the weekend. It meant that – both psychologically and literally – you no longer needed to wear makeup.

We are capable of making decisions not just from the brain but also in our hearts and guts with the combination of chemicals and hormones and countless neurons firing in our bodies at any given second (I wrote about this in my last book, *Shift the Work*). We need an organizational structure that welcomes this kind of whole-body intelligence.

The workplace has been fueled by inadequacy. Inadequate money, ownership, and status cause people to operate from a place of having to prove something. And fast forward, an entire life has been spent trying to disprove the idea of not having enough, doing enough, or being enough.

What would the world look like if people came together from the place of knowing that they are, in fact, enough?

Stepping Out of the Triangle

People lose their sense of personal sovereignty when they are run by fear. Once we feel threatened, we believe it's okay to do anything we want to others. The more we gather in collective fear, the more everyone pledges loyalty to be unified in the fight against the common enemy. This fosters an "us versus them" mentality.

The consequence of this way of thinking, whether in a personal relationship or an organization, is called the *drama triangle*, which was developed by Steven Karpman.[10]

He defines three positions within the triangle: victim, rescuer, and persecutor. Karpman says the movement from one of these positions to another defines the entire terrain of power play.

As soon as anyone claims the victim position ("You did this to me"), it means there are only two seats left at the table: the persecutor and the rescuer. You are forced to either assume the identity of the bad guy who caused harm or the benevolent rescuer who can make it all okay.

People will play into this triangle, thinking they're generating power but they are really just recycling the same issues over and over again. The way out of this triangle is to give rich attention and appreciation to yourself, befriending your feelings and your fear. When you can make friends with fear, it can turn into creative juice. All fear and feelings must be felt to evolve.

The central question to stepping out of power games and to regaining sovereignty is, "What is it you really want to create?" If you ask this question of another person, you can follow it by asking, "How can I support you in getting what you need moving forward toward what you really want?"

That question communicates, "I'm affected by your presence and your desire, and I want to collaborate with you."

We're creating a culture together where everyone can move toward what they really want. We can contribute from authentic power and authenticity rather than fighting for the victim role and blaming others.

What Is Your Intention?

The first step in returning to sovereignty is to restore creativity to the situation. What is the story you have made up about what happened?

Given the result, what was your initial intention? This is a question you can ask yourself as well as others. "What is the step you could take right away toward creating the outcome you really want?"

Of course, in order to be able to ask this, you need to have done something to enliven your sense of true north. The difficulty lies in people not really knowing what they want, and the organization has fostered a kind of vacuum.

As long as people feel disconnected from their own values, they will feel dissatisfied and unhappy no matter what.

Look for Any Opportunity for Agency

When we step into an organization, the most common sentiment we hear is, "If only the organization would change" or "If only management would change, everything would work a lot better." You can begin to restore a sense of agency by asking, "How are you cocreating or enabling the thing you're complaining about? What is the lesson here?"

People with agency and sovereignty produce results.

The Pareto principle, commonly known as the 80/20 rule, suggests that a majority of outcomes are often produced by a minority of inputs.[11] This concept, which originated from the observations of Italian economist Vilfredo Pareto in the early 20th century, has been widely applied in business and economics to illustrate how a small portion of effort or resources frequently leads to a large portion of the results.

Although Frederick W. Taylor's efficiency studies in the early 1900s, including his work at Bethlehem Steel, did not specifically articulate the 80/20 rule, his focus on optimizing work processes and improving labor productivity laid foundational principles that align with maximizing efficiency.[12] Additionally, it's a recognized phenomenon in various sectors, including sales, that a disproportionate amount of productivity often comes from a small segment of the workforce.

Exercise Creativity

No matter what context you're working within, you can increase your sense of sovereignty by prioritizing your own creative expression for 10 minutes a day. This means doing something you love such that while you're doing it, time disappears. If you can do this with other people, it works even better. Our consumerist society has been built on devaluing creativity. Instead, we value speed and power, all based on adrenaline. You get an adrenaline hit when you make a big sale, win, or someone else loses.

But that is not sustainable – it's a short acting drug in the system, so you have to constantly go back for more. The act of creating leads to a physical acknowledgment of connection. Just tiny spurts of creativity during your day will shift your entire relationship to your environment.

Elevate Energy

Another way to increase sovereignty is to do anything to turn up the flow of energy in your body. This could include jumping on a trampoline, running, bicycling, or dancing. Deliberately elevating and changing your energetic state will bring forth more creative genius.

The Flow Research Collective, led by pioneers like Steven Kotler and Rian Doris, focuses on the science of flow states – those optimal states of consciousness where we feel our best and perform our best. Kotler and Doris's work emphasizes the transformative potential of accessing flow, revealing it as a gateway to heightened creativity and performance.[13]

To tap into this reservoir of creative genius, one practical approach is to engage in activities that naturally elevate our energy levels. Physical activities such as jumping on a trampoline, running, cycling, or dancing don't just improve our physical well-being; they are also powerful catalysts for entering flow states. By deliberately altering our energetic state through such activities, we unlock a more profound connection with our creativity and intuition.

This emphasis on finding your flow aligns with the broader mission of increasing personal sovereignty. By cultivating conditions conducive to flow, we not only enhance our capacity for innovation and problem-solving but also forge a deeper sense of alignment and purpose in our lives.

Slowing Down

Deliberately slowing down your activities will increase sovereignty. Speed and fear are twins: they both create adrenaline. Cal Newport sheds light on a common scenario: many professionals find themselves handling tasks 20% beyond their comfortable capacity.[14] This slight but persistent overload maintains a constant undercurrent of stress, yet it's sustainable enough to ensnare us for years.

According to Newport, this condition stems from the autonomous nature of knowledge work, where the absence of clear limits leads to an unmanageable influx of tasks. The default response to this problem is to decline additional work only when overwhelmed, a tactic that invariably results in operating in a state of constant excess.

His idea: deliberately reducing our workload to operate 20% below our maximum capacity. This approach entails declining more requests and allowing ourselves the freedom to end workdays earlier or indulge in leisurely afternoons. His preliminary insight suggests that focusing on deep, meaningful work while efficiently managing administrative duties could mean that the impact of working less is far less significant than we might fear.

Express Appreciation

In a fast-paced hypermasculine environment that emphasizes a war-like atmosphere, running on emergencies and high speed, our language tends to emphasize criticism. We don't have time to be nice. The conscious expression of appreciation reverses that habit.

Drs. John and Julie Gottman emphasize that you need a 5-to-1 ratio of appreciation to criticism to have a successful relationship with anyone, and you have to start with yourself.[15] Once you're in the habit of appreciating yourself, and you get fully comfortable with receiving appreciation, you become like a reservoir, and it enables you to appreciate other people as well.

A culture of appreciation makes it much easier for people to give and receive feedback and learn together without feeling personally attacked: you are primarily valued for who you are, and that is communicated frequently. Once that is in place, we can keep improving on how we do things together.

Talk About Power

The best place to start with shifting an organization to greater shared sovereignty and cocreation is to put the conversation about power on the table. When we can recognize imbalance of power as the default state, then we can all work together toward eradicating it.

I experience this with my daughter when we play basketball. This is not only a game where we are passing back and forth; we put our hands together on the basketball to create a sense of mutual understanding and mutual agreement. This is a "we game," not a "me against you" game.

Equally, I could ask her what she wants to eat when she gets home. She might say "cookies," but I get a chance to respond with questions about healthy choices rather than dictate what the choices are. We create mutual understanding and mutual agreement. We're working toward collective decisions as a "we game."

What Say You?

1. **Reflect on personal sovereignty:** Think of a recent situation where you felt you were not living according to your own values or principles. What external pressures or internal beliefs influenced your actions? How could you have asserted your personal sovereignty in this situation?

2. **Creative acts as sovereignty:** Identify a routine task or decision you face regularly that you typically approach in a conventional manner. How can you reimagine this task or decision through a creative act that asserts your personal sovereignty? Describe this new approach.

3. **Radical responsibility in action:** Reflect on a challenging circumstance in your life. How can you apply the concept of radical responsibility to this situation? Consider factors within your control and how changing your perspective or actions could influence the outcome or your experience of the situation.

4. **Questioning limits and exploring sovereignty:** Questioning our beliefs about limits can lead to a deeper understanding of our personal sovereignty. Choose a belief or limit you currently hold about your abilities, your potential, or the world. How can you challenge this belief? Outline a small experiment you can conduct in your life to test the validity of this limit.

5. **Write about a time you took radical responsibility for an outcome. What did you learn from this experience?**

Chapter 5

Equity Unleashed

"I raise up my voice – not so I can shout, but so that those without a voice can be heard . . . we cannot succeed when half of us are held back."

— Malala Yousafzai

Part 1: Good for One, Good for All

In 1968, amidst a backdrop of upheaval, innovation, and trials, the line between life and death was discovered to lie within the crucial first hour following trauma. Dr. R. Adams Cowley wasn't just any physician; he was a visionary. He brought the "golden hour" concept into the spotlight, emphasizing the overlooked yet critical importance of those initial 60 minutes for survival. His revolutionary approach? Swiftly transporting trauma victims to advanced medical care via military helicopters.

By 1970, Cowley's ambitions had expanded. He envisioned a Maryland where top-tier medical care was accessible to all, not as a privilege but as a fundamental right. Realizing this dream, however, was far from easy, especially with his proposal for state funding. Cowley knew he needed a Navy SEAL–like team of warriors to bring his vision to fruition. Through what he termed *voluntary cooperation*, he managed to unite an unlikely coalition of doctors and government bureaucrats.

Imagine the challenge of aligning such a diverse group toward a common goal, voluntarily. It's like getting cats and dogs to break bread together.

Dr. Cowley didn't just create a vision; he built bridges, found common ground, and fostered a culture of enthusiasm over obligation. His ability to unite disparate forces under a shared mission was nothing short of remarkable.

The University of Maryland Medical Center Shock Trauma now boasts a 95% success rate, a testament to Cowley's enduring legacy of innovation, collaboration, and unwavering commitment to saving lives.

How do I know? Because they counted me in that percentage once.

Before I share how I landed in Shock Trauma and to understand the gravity of that moment, you need to grasp the rugged terrain that was my life back then.

In high school, I was a big fish in a small pond, an all-state athlete among a tight-knit team of 27. Fast forward to college, and suddenly, I was 1 among 90 – each as good as or better than me. It was a humbling transition from high school hero to feeling like a college zero.

But the real challenge for me was the juggling act. Academics at Hopkins were like dodging bullets, and on the side, I was running a general contracting business that had ballooned to 150 college kids painting houses under my watch. Weekends after football, I'd switch from athlete to cook, then bartender, never pausing, always hustling.

And then there was my mom. Her health battles cast a long shadow over these years – two kidney transplants, two pancreas transplants, legal blindness, and life in a wheelchair. My responsibilities to her added layers of complexity to an already packed life.

Football, which should have been a refuge, became another checkbox. Instead of dedicating myself to workouts and film sessions, I was just going through the motions, my heart and mind scattered across my many obligations.

Yet, amidst this whirlwind, there was a moment during a game in my senior year when something shifted. Amidst the chaos and struggle, I found a spark of desire to reconnect, to make a play, to reclaim a piece of myself that felt lost in the shuffle. It was a fleeting thought, a whisper of ambition, but it was there – the urge to plug back in and make a difference on the field.

The stadium was alive, a pulsating hub of raw energy, echoing with the screams of fans caught up in the excitement of the game. And there we were, faced with a nail-biting fourth down with two yards to go. The air was thick with anticipation, every heartbeat in the crowd syncing up as we all waited for what would happen next.

This was the moment that could define everything – a test of determination and skill, where every second counted.

The adrenaline, the passion, the preparation, everything culminated right then. I was the team's shield, the outside linebacker. And as the opposition made their play, every lesson, every practice, every memory surged, pushing me to give my all. So, I slowed down, took a breath, and waited for the play to unfold in the way I could see in my mind. This play was mine.

But fate had other plans.

The details are a bit hazy now, but I remember the moment that changed everything. An off-balance move, and suddenly, the world became a dizzying blur of lights and sounds.

In that critical split second, the running back lowered his head, challenging me with an unstoppable force. My entire football career had drilled into me one rule: "the low man wins."

So, without a second thought for my own safety, I went low, just as I had been taught.

Playing fearlessly in high school, I rarely suffered injuries. But college football was a different beast. My freshman year brought a high ankle sprain that sidelined me for the season, leaving me on crutches for three months.

Sophomore year was marked by a concussion and a wrist surgery that forced me to play with a cast for the next two years.

Junior year came with its own set of challenges: a nagging shoulder injury and turf toe, which I had once dismissed as trivial until I learned how a sprained toe can torment you with every step. That injury never fully healed.

By my senior year, my physical condition was far from ideal. Unlike my high school days of playing both offense and defense without leaving the field, at Hopkins, I was strictly on defense. The lack of conditioning became painfully apparent toward the end of most games.

This game was no exception. Overwhelmed by fatigue, I met the running back head-on, helmet to helmet. The collision was met with a loud pop.

A chilling rush swept over me, leaving me feeling as if I had momentarily left my body. For anyone who's ever been knocked out, you know this feeling. In that instant, I wasn't sure if I was awake, alive, or unconscious.

From the roaring crowds to the hushed tones of medical professionals, my world transformed in a flash. I was headed to Shock Trauma, battling my sixth concussion and a pinched spinal cord.

Strapped to a board and in the back of an ambulance is not exactly how I saw my football career ending.

When I arrived at Shock Trauma, it wasn't lost on me that this was where my mom was for the four years while I was in college. Although there at the exact same time, I chose to keep the accident and our coincidental proximity a secret from her.

The atmosphere inside Shock Trauma was as surreal as it was intense. They ushered me into a large room, where the sounds of other patients filled the space – a stark reminder of the fragility of life.

To my left, an elderly woman was screaming as she battled the aftermath of a fall that left her with a broken hip. On my right, a man groaned under the weight of multiple gunshot wounds; a palpable sense of urgency surrounded him. I would later learn that he didn't survive. Luckily for me, it was just another concussion and a sprained neck – minor in comparison.

These moments of human vulnerability and the swift passage of life left a lasting imprint on my mind. Life, I realized, unfolds in rapid, unpredictable flashes, only to continue its relentless march forward.

The true revelation from this experience was witnessing the medical team operate with steadfast precision and calm amidst the chaos of human suffering. Their actions were not only impressive but profoundly moving, illuminating the resilience and strength of the human spirit.

Part 2: Show Me the Incentive

Have you ever noticed the power imbalance between those paying for services and those providing them? This imbalance is built into all kinds of transactions: having someone cook for you at a restaurant, getting your car serviced, cleaners making sure your house is spotless.

The one paying the money and receiving the service is assumed to have more power than the one providing the service and getting paid.

The customer is seen as the "authority" by virtue of controlling the payment. "Authority bias" manifests in the assumption that the customer, as the payer, has the final say and superior judgment over the service being provided.

This can influence the behavior and perceptions of the service provider, who may feel compelled to defer to the customer's wishes, and the customer, who may feel entitled to special treatment or compliance.

In the context of job interviews, the interaction inherently involves a power dynamic that can significantly influence the behavior and perceptions of both parties. For the interviewee, there's often a sense of vulnerability and a need to impress, stemming from the desire to secure the position.

This can lead to natural feelings of nervousness, self-doubt, and a need to seek the hiring manager's approval. The interviewee might overemphasize their accomplishments or downplay their weaknesses in an effort to align with what they believe the hiring manager wants to hear.

On the other side of the table, the hiring manager holds the authority in this scenario, guiding the conversation and evaluating the candidate's suitability for the role. This position of power comes from their ability to make decisions that can significantly affect the interviewee's career.

But in this kind of power imbalance, both parties lose. Both become less authentic, less creative, and less connected than they would be in a normal, non-transactional human interaction.

The Haves and Have Nots

The most obvious symptom of power imbalance in the workplace is financial inequity, reflected in the ratio between the lowest and highest paid worker. George Zimmer, the founder of Men's Wearhouse, was one of the first CEOs to take a stand in the late 1990s by establishing a 1 to 20 limit on the pay disparity between the lowest and highest paid workers.[1] This means if the lowest paid worker was getting $10 per hour, the CEO would max out at $200 per hour.

A more recent example, but with a twist, is Dan Price of Gravity Payments. Price made headlines in 2015 when he announced he would slash his own salary from about $1 million to $70,000 and set $70,000 as the minimum salary for all his employees.[2] This move was a signal that he trusts his team. It was about lifting everyone to a living wage that respected their contributions.

The result? A surge in productivity, employee loyalty, and profitability that turned the traditional pay disparity debate on its head. Price's approach is leading by example, not explanation.

This move, steeped in the belief that everyone deserves a fair share, serves as an amazing example, with quantifiable benefits, for others pondering the balance between equity and profitability. Both Zimmer and Price challenged the status quo, urging a reevaluation of the value we place on work and the people who do it, pushing the conversation about pay disparity into new territories. It's a heartening sight, showcasing that, indeed, change is possible, and sometimes, it starts with a single decision to do things differently.

We tend to accept this kind of differential of income in some contexts more than others. One of the most frequently cited examples of massive financial inequity are Amazon and Tesla, where Jeff Bezos and Elon Musk are worth several hundred billion dollars, but a warehouse worker or someone answering phones is just scraping by. The average person finds this massive differential offensive.

But less offensive is Taylor Swift making millions for one concert, or Tom Cruise earning $100 million for one movie, while the people who clean the concert venue or movie theater are earning minimum wage.

Why do you think that is?

> "A nation that continues year after year to spend more money on military defense than on programs of social uplift is approaching spiritual death."
>
> — *Martin Luther King Jr.*

This gap in financial equity is simply unsustainable. If we were to keep heading in this direction, we would eventually return to the same conditions as feudalism or monarchy.

Similar to the national debt in America – it simply cannot keep increasing forever. Back in 1929, the US owed $20 billion in Treasury bonds, or 16% of the GDP, which was already seen at the time as a problem without any solution in sight.[3]

In 2023, that figure is $34 trillion, 125% of the GDP, and approximately 1,500 times what it was less than 100 years before.[4] How much longer can that situation last before it implodes? Some economists say as little as 5 or 10 years. The situation will, at some point, require a quantum leap into a completely different kind of financial system.

The same is true of the equity imbalance in the workplace: it cannot keep expanding forever. At some point, we are going to have to find a different way of collaborating and creating things together.

Why not now? Who says we have to wait?

Kinds of Equity

Imbalance of income and assets is only one way of measuring inequity in the workplace. There are also the various perks associated with power: the corner office, the convenient parking space, the expense account, and the freedom to make decisions and choose what you do with your time are all also meaningful kinds of equity.

For those in power, there is access to pleasurable, enjoyable experiences, the freedom to travel to different parts of the world, and the opportunity to reflect at leisure, think about your ideas, and actualize your vision. You have access to "mastermind groups," people, and connections you otherwise wouldn't, and open doors that are shut for others.

How dirty you are expected to get in the course of performing your duties, and the degree to which you are required to risk your life or your health through exposure to danger or toxic substances, are also important differentials.

Equally, the ways you feel respected, acknowledged, looked up to – the opportunities for a positive self-image – are other forms of equity. This also includes the opportunity to create a legacy, make decisions and feel committed to actions you can be proud of and that can be an inspiration to your children and future generations.

The example we find the most meaningful in examining organizational structure, however, has to do with inequity of opportunity for innovation. This means evaluating not only how much different stakeholders are receiving but also how much money, perks, and other benefits they each have to contribute and express their latent gifts.

Obviously, if someone is working for minimum wage, struggling to put food on their table and pay medical bills, let alone pay for a quality education, while the CEO owns multiple homes and flies in a private jet, there is something imbalanced about the situation.

But, if a potentially creative human being is only given automated tasks to perform, never asked their opinion about what matters to them, never given an opportunity to be creative or to make an original contribution, that may be an equal kind of tragedy engendered by what we consider normal in the workplace.

Elon Musk can dream of populating Mars and then take real steps to make his dream come true. If someone on the production line in one of his factory's dreams of greater access to higher education for inner city youth, they might not have the same opportunities to make it real.

By centralizing opportunities for innovation at the top of the pyramid, we reduce our capacity to integrate complementary ways of seeing complex problems. So, it is not just that Elon Musk and Jeff Bezos win and the lowest paid workers lose. Everybody loses.

We lose all the contributions other members of the organization could have made. By centralizing power and financial equity, we also centralize meaning and creativity, and we let the narrative for the future be created by the person with the loudest voice and the biggest bank balance.

In writing this book and talking to so many intelligent people about these topics, it's difficult to not think about the words in the Declaration of Independence. In 1776, Thomas Jefferson penned, "We hold these truths to be self-evident, that all men are created equal, that they are endowed by their Creator with certain unalienable Rights, that among these are Life, Liberty and the pursuit of Happiness."

Maybe it is time for an upgrade to *"every human being has the unalienable right to have the opportunity to express their innate genius."*

The Risk-Reward Ratio

These kinds of dramatic equity imbalances are often justified by the notion of the "risk-reward ratio." This is the premise that built the American Dream. We've come to understand if you work hard, build something valuable, and take risks, you may fail and face ruin. But with the right mixture of tenacity, strategy, and luck, you may win and be tremendously rewarded.

The ratio between risk and reward is experienced differently depending on where you function within the imbalanced system. The founder or CEO, sitting on massive personal assets and the capacity to borrow money from wealthy investors, has a completely different relationship to risk and reward than someone working paycheck to paycheck with accumulated debt.

And this gives zero attribution to all the many other cofactors of success. Where you were born, when, and to whom.

> "You are not a product of your environment, but of your expectations."
>
> — *Wes Moore, governor of Maryland*

For someone without assets or access to investment, the notion of risk and reward is very different. As long as your basic survival is on the line, you're not going to take the same kind of risks in expressing your true north.

The risk-reward ratio is often used to justify this kind of imbalance of equity, particularly financial equity. If you risk your capital, you are entitled to the spoils.

Thinking in a deeply disruptive way about work and organizations, consider that there are many other kinds of risks people can take and many rewards they can gain. The more we broaden our understanding of risk and reward, the more nuanced and multidimensional our understanding of how a healthy living organization might operate becomes.

Of course, we can risk money, which is the most common metric. We can also risk spending our valuable time devoted to something that might or might not bear fruit. We can also risk expressing daring ideas, which are important to us.

If you express something you deeply believe in or care about, and it is laughed at or dismissed, it can be even more devastating than losing cash. We take a risk every time we devote our attention to something meaningful – a big reason why people don't choose to think disruptively.

If you put your energy into a job that doesn't mean much to you, you are going to earn your salary, go home each day to your family and hobbies, and leave your work behind.

If you dedicate yourself to something you really care about, whether it's art, the environment, social justice, or making a better world, you've got much more on the line. The success or failure of those pursuits will be much more significant than what happens at a job you don't really care about. You risk much more significantly every time you allow yourself to dream in a way that arouses your sense of contribution.

By taking a risk that pans out, you can be rewarded with a sense of dignity, feel good about yourself, and know your life has meaning and purpose. You can be rewarded with the opportunity to be creative, to turn vision into reality. Taking a risk that pans out can reward you with subjective experiences of joy, freedom, and even love. In order to understand all of the different kinds of equity at stake and the risk-reward ratio that governs each of them, we need to be able to zoom out from "business as usual."

For many people, it's only on their deathbed, in a near-death experience, or a psychedelic journey that they let go of our usual preoccupations enough to recognize the other kinds of equity that govern our lives besides money.

Can Artificial Intelligence (AI) Unlock a New Era of Humanness, Creativity, and Equity?

"We shape our buildings, and then our buildings shape us."

— Winston Churchill

The looming prospect of AI-induced job displacement, with some forecasts suggesting up to 40% of current roles could be automated by 2030, certainly stirs anxiety. Yet, history reminds us our tango with technology has deep roots.

Reflecting on a century's shift, an article from the *Atlantic* notes that in 1910, about a third of the US population – 38 million people – were deeply entrenched in agriculture. By 1950, this number had decreased to just 10%, and by 2010, it stood at a mere 2%, despite an exponential increase in food production.[5]

What seemed like a potential disaster turned into an opportunity for unprecedented efficiency and growth. Machines didn't bring about the end times; they opened the door to new possibilities.

I hold an optimistic view on AI's potential to elevate human creativity to new heights. Just as the technological advancements of the past liberated us from the drudgery of physical labor, AI has the potential to free us from the confines of rote and repetitive tasks, granting us the space to engage more deeply with our creative impulses.

AI embodies the potential to enhance our creative capacities rather than diminish our roles. It marks a new chapter, offering an opportunity to redefine our approach to work, creativity, and collective achievement.

As organizations navigate through these transformative times, AI's role becomes increasingly pivotal. From administrative functions to design, AI's integration across various sectors suggests a move toward more strategic and creative endeavors. This evolution, however, prompts critical reflections on the future of work, equity, and the essence of creativity in an AI-enhanced world.

Andrew Yang was one of the early voices of this evolving discourse on the future of work. His presidential campaign brought to the forefront the critical issue of job displacement due to automation and AI. Yang's proposal for a universal basic income, named the *freedom dividend*, aimed to provide a financial safety net for all Americans, focusing a proactive approach to the economic shifts anticipated with technological progress.

Although acknowledging AI's potential to exacerbate existing inequalities initially, Professor Scott Galloway also sees it as a conduit for greater prosperity, driven by enhanced efficiency and innovation. His cautious yet optimistic perspective suggests that with strategic integration of AI, businesses can achieve more equitable and creative outcomes.[6]

Galloway anticipates hearing this line from CEO's more often in the future, "We're going to be a smaller company that does more business, thanks to AI."

The integration of AI into our workplaces and lives poses an opportunity to fundamentally rethink our approaches to work, creativity, and collaboration. This could be one of the biggest human unlocks – freeing up the very thing we all want more of: time and creative opportunity. AI has the potential to be the great equalizer in workplace power imbalances, giving everyone an equal opportunity to lean into their innate genius.

We are confronted with a pivotal choice: to view AI as an existential threat or as a key to unlocking a future brimming with potential. The promise of AI extends beyond operational gains to include a reimagined future where every individual has the freedom to explore their creative and intellectual potential, making the most of our time in this universe.

Redefining Equity: The Blockchain Revolution

The rapid evolution of technology brings more to the forefront than just AI. The landscape of equity stands at the threshold of transformative change, fueled by the emerging capabilities of blockchain technology. This advancement goes beyond mere technical intricacies, holding the vision to ignite levels of collective action and empowerment that were previously unimaginable.

When talking about structural power imbalances, blockchain technology cracks that wide open. Blockchain projects a future where power and resource distribution are decentralized, challenging the traditional, centralized modes of authority. This development resonates with the increasing demand for a fairer world, compelling us to rethink notions of ownership, governance, and participation in today's digital era.

A prime example of blockchain's disruptive potential is its application in cryptocurrencies. The stark contrast between conventional fiat currencies and digital alternatives like Bitcoin showcases blockchain's capacity to revolutionize the concept of equity. This paradigm shift prompts a reevaluation of currency essence, financial autonomy, and the possibility of crafting a financial system that inclusively serves the broader society.

A notable use case was the November 2021 ConstitutionDAO endeavor. This initiative sought to harness the decentralized nature of blockchain to bid for an original copy of the US Constitution at a Sotheby's auction. Through the Ethereum blockchain, ConstitutionDAO quickly raised more than $40 million globally, with contributors receiving tokens that provided a stake in the collective's decision-making process and possible ownership of the historic document.[7]

Although ConstitutionDAO did not win the auction, the attempt highlighted blockchain's potential to rally communities around shared goals, challenging traditional power structures and governance models. The initiative marked a pivotal moment in digital cooperation and collective ambition discussions, sparking dialogue on how decentralized autonomous organizations might play a role in realizing common societal and cultural goals.

The examples of ConstitutionDAO and the broader implications of blockchain and cryptocurrencies serve as compelling evidence of technology's ability to dismantle established power hierarchies and enhance equity. This technology foretells a future of democratized governance and ownership, where communities and individuals possess the agency to collaboratively forge their futures.

In this transformative period, blockchain compels us to reexamine our approaches to equity, authority, and cooperation. It provides the foundation for creating transparent, secure, and inclusive systems, aligning with the core of the who says? ethos of challenging the prevailing order and championing a world where collective engagement and benefits are paramount.

Questioning Ownership

In discussions with people who are looking at organizations in a deeply disruptive way, I found the very notion of ownership itself is underlying these assumptions about the distribution of equity. We take it so deeply for granted that to even question notions of ownership causes alarm. "What, are you a Marxist? Are you asking me to live in a hippie commune?"

Out of 5.6 plus million species on this planet, we are unique in that we believe everything must have an owner. You own your house, your car, and the land on which the house is built. If that land has trees growing on it, you own the trees.

What if a deer wanders through your backyard? Do you own it? What if a bird makes a nest in your tree, do you own the bird, the nest, and the eggs? If one of those eggs hatched and went to live in a neighbor's tree, is that abandonment? Theft? We own our pets and thankfully have at least drawn the line on owning other human beings.

These unexamined assumptions about ownership, and therefore about theft, still leave many terrains unclaimed. When European settlers first came to North America, they tried to make deals with the Indigenous people. They offered shiny colored beads in exchange for hundreds of acres.

The Indigenous people thought this was a great deal to get these bright shiny beads. "And what do I have to give up to have them? Nothing! The land belongs to itself." The equivalent today might be if someone approached you and said, "I'll give you this beautiful golden object in exchange for the bit of the sky that you see from out your window."

All these arbitrary notions we share about ownership translate into the way we think about creative equity in the workplace. We think we own ideas in the same way we assumed we could own land. Buffalo and bison live together in the wild.

No one says, "This is my patch, and this is yours." The same land is accessible to everyone. Hardwired into all Native American culture is the recognition that whenever you use a resource from the land, it is just borrowed, and it will have to be returned.

We have to see brilliant ideas in the same way. Having a great and original idea, particularly since the technological revolution, defines who wins and loses. But where do ideas really come from? Do they really come from *you*, as a localized entity?

By thinking of creativity, innovation, and vision as forms of equity to be owned, we give brilliance access to the same scarcity game.

We create an imbalance of financial equity within the organization. We operate under the assumption that there's only so much and 'I must get mine before you get yours.' There are only so many VIP parking spaces, corner offices, and golf club memberships.

We think about creative equity in the same way. "This is my idea. It came from *me*. There are only so many good ideas to go around." By creating scarcity around the capacity to innovate, we shut down innovation within most of the organization and centralize it at the top of a pyramid of power.

In Rick Rubin's book, *The Creative Act: A Way of Being*, he puts it beautifully: "Turning something from an idea into a reality can make it seem smaller. It changes from unearthly to earthly. The imagination has no limits. The physical world does. The work exists in both."[8]

What Do We Value?

In his book *Counterfeit Gods: The Empty Promise of Money, Sex, and Power, and the Only Hope That Matters*, Timothy Keller presents a succinct history of the American dream.[9] Even back in the 1700s, Americans had an unbridled desire to chase opportunity. Often escaping from oppressive monarchies in Europe, they had a craving to make things their own.

To create things, Keller points out, we've been chasing and climbing and consuming for 250 years, and many people find themselves empty at the end. He calls these hollow goals *counterfeit gods*. It means we are using the wrong metric to measure our lives and, particularly, the way we work.

In his book, *Chasing the Scream: The First and Last Days of the War on Drugs*, Johann Hari reflects on the Rat Park experiment done in the 1960s.[10] Many rats were put in a cage and provided with two different feeding bottles. One just had water, and the other one was supplemented with cocaine. As long as the cage was empty, the rats would almost invariably drink the cocaine and get the dopamine hit. Hari reports this experiment was repeated recently under slightly different circumstances and with a notably different outcome. This time, the rats were put into a kind of rat utopia, where there were plenty of toys to play with and just the right number of other rats to feel social without overcrowding.

It turns out, the rats were no longer interested in the water with cocaine. Even after having tried it once, they would refuse the solution in favor of the bottle with just water. This finding has revolutionized the way we think about addiction. Instead of creating environments based on money and positions of power, which are something like counterfeit gods, we need to start thinking about organizations built around allowing people meaning and purpose in their lives. Then just like the rats with the cocaine, they might no longer be interested in playing with power.

In Chapter 6, we're going to explore why a sense of meaning and purpose might be the most valuable metrics for people to feel engaged in to come together in organizations, and how it is always an inside job.

What Say You?

1. **Reflect on a time of unity:** Think of a moment when you witnessed or were part of a group overcoming significant differences to achieve a common goal. What bridged the gap between diverse perspectives, and how can this lesson apply more broadly to societal challenges?

2. **Assessing the power dynamics:** In your daily interactions, where do you see the power imbalance between service provider and consumer? How does recognizing this imbalance change your perspective or behavior in these situations?

3. **Innovation for all:** Consider a situation where a less-heard member of a team or community had a groundbreaking idea. How was this idea received, and what could have been done to foster an environment more open to such contributions from all levels?

Chapter 6

The Market Never Sleeps

"The price of anything is the amount of life you exchange for it."
— Henry David Thoreau

Part 1: For the Love of the Game

The pressure to perform is real. I have been hustling since I was 13 years old, working weekends, side gigs, hustles, and anything and everything to make enough money to give me the freedom and flexibility to make the choices I didn't have.

In the grand scheme of life, each decision weaves a golden thread that contributes to the ultimate design of our personal and professional existence. This journey is about more than the hustle; it's about discovering the why behind the grind, the deeper calling that drives us to push beyond our limits.

The path to self-discovery often intersects with our professional journeys, leading us down roads paved with uncertainty, ambition, and a relentless pursuit of something more. My venture into management consulting at the young age of 23 was not just a career choice; it was a leap off a cliff into the vast unknown, guided by a mix of desperation, divine intervention, and a dash of audacity.

Two weeks after the neck injury that sent me to Shock Trauma (see Chapter 5), I had my first (and last) job interview with the (at the time) prestigious Anderson Consulting. Still a little loopy from the concussion, I entered the room with my neck brace on and ready for just about anything.

The interviewer said: "Wow, you poor thing, what happened to your neck?"

I said, "I just ended my football career at Shock Trauma with a pinched spinal cord and my sixth concussion."

The interviewer took a second, and just said, "Wow, that's terrible!"

I went on to say I was not completely with it, and she might have to ask me the questions more than once.

She asked me about my story.

I started,

It may not be obvious, but for the past three years, while at Hopkins, I have been running a small house painting company that grew from 5 to 150 people in that time. I learned how to cold-call, market door-to-door, book mall and trade shows to generate leads, and found interesting ways to guerrilla market with lawn signs, swag, and just anything I could get my hands on to build the business.

Beyond this, I also hired a lot of college students. With a fairly high turnover at first, I learned the game of business: if you treat employees like clients and clients like employees, you create an easy, simple, rarely complicated culture where everyone feels like a stakeholder.

And then you have to imagine the hundreds of homes we painted. These were people's homes, their number one investment, their top priority. We were not professionals in the trade, in this for the long term, but college kids earning money for college.

So we used that line: "we are not here just to paint your house but to help pay for our future." It helped the homeowners understand we were also vested in something long term by just telling the truth.

This did not mean mistakes and problems didn't happen. In fact, they happened daily. I became really good at problem-solving, critical thinking, being strategic, and finding a way to gain agreement from multiple people in a single encounter.

She continued to say, "Wow . . ."

All of this boded well in this interview.

The interview was a bit overwhelming. Starting fresh off a visit to Shock Trauma and still nursing the effects, I continued, sharing small bits about taking care of my sick mom and my story of getting to Hopkins.

Life's pivotal moments often arrive unannounced, dressed in adversity and leading us to crossroads that define our path forward. My interview with Anderson Consulting, marked by vulnerability and resilience, was more than an evaluation of my potential; it was another test of my potentializing my whole self in the face of immense fear.

At the time, I had no idea, but getting an offer to work at Accenture was rare. I believe they only offered five jobs per campus. After a few of these interviews, I was offered a job and accepted.

A signing bonus, a set salary, benefits, travel, working inside businesses, and solving even bigger problems sounded like precisely the fit for me.

Until it didn't.

During the pre-onboarding, Anderson put me up at the Ritz in DC, which was my first experience in a real fancy hotel.

The bed felt like it was for the richy-rich. The mini bar was stocked, I could live there for a month.

I remember wearing the robe all night, ordering room service for the first time in my life, and feeling as though I had arrived again . . . until I hadn't.

Something just felt off. Being with the folks there, I just got this sense I truly didn't belong. I was afraid they would "find me out."

They all walked the same and dressed the same: in khakis, a button-up white shirt, and brown shoes. Everyone talked the same way as if they were making these people in the back with some cloning machine.

I started to freak out.

A few weeks before I was to begin this next chapter at Anderson Consulting, my painting business was going through it.

My business was part of a larger franchise and there were problems at the corporate level I wasn't aware of. One day, the company was unable to meet its obligations. I had a group of guys painting a mansion near the Johns Hopkins campus, and when they found out what was happening with the company, and that they most likely weren't getting paid, they decided to take matters into their own hands.

They trashed the mansion, broke windows, threw black oil-based paint all over the place, and left it a wreck.

The homeowner, Stan Burns, was understandably upset. He tried to get company officials to fix the damage but just got the runaround. I went to see Stan and reassured him I would send a new crew over to make repairs the following week, and I'd pay them out of my own pocket. He refused.

"No, I want you to fix it," Stan said. "You, personally."

Me? Personally? Was this guy crazy?

I was only running this business; I didn't know how to paint! I told Stan, and I also told him I was scheduled to fly out of Baltimore in a few days to start a new job at one of the top consulting firms in the nation. Stan was unmoved. He insisted I take personal responsibility for righting the mess my crew had made.

Well, what else could I do? I had to keep my word.

So, I showed up at Stan's house bright and early the next morning and went to work. My progress was so slow, and I had to postpone the start of my new job. I labored several hours each day for a couple of weeks when one afternoon around lunchtime, Stan popped into the room where I was working and invited me to go out for a sandwich.

It was from that point on that I was given yet another gift from the universe in this kind soul's time and insight. He took me under his wing and shared his philosophies on life and business. We talked about how to be a good man, a good husband, and a good father.

Stan would say, *"You've got to love who you work with and love who you do the work for. That's the kind of passion that breeds success."*

Stan helped me see, I was an outdoor cat, likely not very employable in the traditional sense. Stan opened my eyes to that. In granting me permission to break the rules and adjust my aspirations, he gave me an incredible gift.

About six months later, I met the partner with whom I started entreQuest, now, SHIFT, and the rest, as they say, is history. Stan was a generous person whose wisdom and encouragement changed the trajectory of my life forever.

Sadly, before we started the company, Stan suddenly passed away, just two months before my mom that same year. I think about him often and still have a picture on my desk his family gave to me of him running on the beach. He loved the game of life and gave me a great example to follow.

Part 2: It's Not Personal, It's Just Business

Do you remember "market day" from the Introduction? The Thursday afternoons when everybody had the best of everything to sell and applied persuasive tactics to convince you?

Persuasion and manipulation eclipsed truthfulness and honesty in the marketplace. At the end of the day, everybody would go home, not thinking about money or transactions for the rest of the week. After the Industrial Revolution and with the advent of factories, we became able to produce things in much larger quantities, and then we needed to sell them.

So, what's the best way to get people to buy things? Tell them they are not enough without your product or service. Tell them what they need more of, even if they don't.

We are generations removed from the Greatest Generation, when they didn't throw away plastic bags, instead reusing them because they didn't have excess. By comparison, our concept of materialism today says we need the next iPhone 15 because the camera might work a little better.

In the shadow of our ancestors' frugality and resourcefulness lies a modern paradox: the insatiable quest for the latest, often unnecessary, technological marvels. This juxtaposition challenges us to reconsider our definitions of necessity and luxury, urging a return to mindfulness about the environmental and psychological costs of unchecked materialism.

Today, some shops are open seven days a week, and the marketplace is active 24/7 via the internet. We are glued to devices, continuously shouting advertising slogans at us and never letting us escape the marketplace. We live permanently trapped in a transactional mindset.

The win-at-all-costs mentality is finally starting to crack. The idea that human nature is to transact with each other is not our natural state. Business is personal.

This conversation about the inherent personal nature of business and the indispensable roles of trust and authenticity continues to evolve, emphasized by findings from the 2023 Edelman Trust Barometer. This latest report illuminates an accelerating trend: society's demand for businesses to prioritize ethical leadership and societal contribution alongside profitability.[1]

The data is compelling, revealing an overwhelming 86% of respondents expect CEOs to publicly speak out on societal challenges, from health crises to economic disparities and climate change. This marks a significant shift toward viewing businesses as agents of change, capable of driving societal progress in collaboration with, or in some cases, in the absence of government action.

Moreover, the barometer highlights a growing consensus among the global populace that businesses have a duty not only to their shareholders but to a broader set of stakeholders, including their employees, communities, and the environment. This expanded view of corporate responsibility reflects a deeper understanding of the interconnectedness of business performance and societal health.

Such insights create a clear signal for businesses to redefine their missions and operations in alignment with these evolving expectations. It's a call to action for leaders to forge a new path that integrates profit with purpose, ensuring their companies not only thrive economically but also contribute positively to the fabric of society.

The survey also highlights a pivotal shift in the workforce's expectations, with employees seeking more from their employers than just a paycheck. They crave a workplace where their values are reflected and where they can contribute to the greater good. It's a call for businesses to operate transparently and ethically, fostering a culture where employees feel valued not just for their labor but also for their humanity.

Reflecting on my own experiences, the essence of trust and mutual respect was a cornerstone of the environments I thrived in.

Whether it was navigating the complexities of a startup or steering through the challenges of corporate restructuring, the moments where leadership demonstrated genuine care and commitment to ethical practices were the moments that inspired the highest levels of performance and loyalty among teams.

This parallels the culture I experienced growing up, where bonds were forged not in boardrooms but in shared struggles on the street. The principle remains the same: when individuals feel supported, seen, and valued for their contributions and as people, they are more inclined to invest their energy, creativity, and loyalty. This is the bedrock of high-performing teams and ethical business practices.

One of my business partners, Jeff Cherry, is building one of the first venture capital firms run entirely on this idea. Starting in 2015, Jeff saw the disparity and opportunity in female and diverse founders and believed that talent was equally distributed, but opportunity was not.

I quickly got involved in the general partnership as an investor and mentor of Conscious Ventures Lab/Partnership, which is now called the Novella Center for Entrepreneurship. I have watched Jeff not just raise more than $20 million and invest 70% into female and diverse founders but also turn the hearts and minds of so many who once viewed this as an insignificant idea. He is a true inspiration.

In an era where technology has made interactions increasingly impersonal, remembering the human element – the stories, aspirations, and vulnerabilities behind each email, project, or transaction – becomes paramount. As leaders, fostering an environment where psychological safety is a priority and where being authentic is valued over conforming to a corporate persona can transform the workplace from a mere business transaction into a community of purpose-driven individuals.

Thus, the adage "It's just business" becomes increasingly obsolete. Business, in its truest form, is about human connections and mutual exchange of value and progress. It's about building a legacy of integrity, purpose, and trust. As we navigate the future of work, let us not forget that at the heart of every transaction, strategy, and innovation are people – each with their own stories, dreams, and the inherent need to belong and contribute to something greater than themselves.

"It's business" is an excuse to be a jerk. Full stop.

In the pursuit of success, the line between personal sacrifice and professional gain is often blurred. This is profoundly illustrated in the lives of two executives I worked with, whose journeys to the apex of their careers were marked by profound realizations about the true nature of success.

Success at What Cost

Let's first delve into the life of John (name changed for privacy), who served as the COO of a $3.7 billion corporation. His career was a portrait of conventional success: rapid ascensions, accolades, and the respect of his peers. John's days were a whirlwind of meetings, decisions, and constant travel. He was the embodiment of the corporate dream, yet his personal life told a different story.

John's dedication to his career came at a hefty price. His marriage crumbled under the weight of his absence, and his relationships with his children were strained, reduced to brief phone calls and occasional visits. Friendships and hobbies fell by the wayside, sacrificed at the altar of professional ambition.

The turning point came unexpectedly. John was gently nudged toward early retirement during a routine business lunch – a euphemism for being replaced. At that moment, as he looked at me across the table, his eyes mirrored a profound realization.

"I gave my whole life, wasted it, and ruined every major relationship in the name of work," he confessed. The cost of his success was not measured in dollars, but in the years of life he had exchanged for it.

John's story echoes Henry David Thoreau's poignant words in Walden: "The cost of a thing is the amount of what I will call life, which is required to be exchanged for it, immediately or in the long run."[2] John had paid dearly, and now, at the twilight of his career, he was left to reckon with the true price of his achievements.

The Reflection of Mandela's Daughter

The narrative of Nelson Mandela's daughter, as reported, offers a parallel of personal sacrifice in the pursuit of a greater cause. Mandela, a global icon for freedom and justice, was absent for much of his children's lives due to his imprisonment and political commitments. His daughter candidly expressed the personal cost of her father's monumental journey – the absence of a father figure during her formative years.

This story, though different in context, resonates with the same theme: the inescapable trade-off between personal sacrifices and the pursuit of something greater, be it professional success or a noble cause.

The Second Executive's Journey

Another executive I worked with, Sianna, climbed the corporate ladder in the high-stakes world of finance. Her career was a relentless pursuit of excellence, marked by long hours, intense pressure, and a single-minded focus on success. Sianna's rise was meteoric, shattering glass ceilings and earning her a spot in the boardroom of a major financial institution.

However, Sianna's success also came at a cost. Her health suffered under relentless stress, and her personal life was a series of missed moments and strained relationships. She often joked about her office being her true home, but beneath the humor lay a stark reality – her personal identity was indistinguishable from her professional persona.

A health scare forced Sianna to pause and reflect. In a moment of vulnerability, she admitted, "I've climbed to the top, only to realize I've been climbing the wrong mountain." This epiphany was a catalyst for change. Sianna began to reevaluate her priorities, seeking a balance that had eluded her for years.

A Reckoning with Success

Both John's and Sianna's stories are a powerful testament to the complexity of success. Their experiences force us to question the conventional metrics of success and the sacrifices we are willing to make in its pursuit. They remind us, success, devoid of personal fulfillment and authentic relationships, can be a hollow achievement.

Their journeys are a call to reflect on our own paths, to consider the full cost of our ambitions, and to find a balance that does not require us to forfeit the essence of who we are. In the relentless pursuit of success, we must not lose sight of what truly matters – our relationships, our well-being, and our authentic selves.

In the spectrum of leadership, there exists a complex interplay between privilege and sacrifice. Occupying a position of influence is indeed a privilege, one that comes with its own unique set of challenges and responsibilities. This truth transcends the confines of corporate boardrooms, touching leaders in all walks of life.

Consider Coach Wrenn. More than my high school football coach, he was a father figure to countless young men, many of whom found a haven from harsh street life on the football field. Coach Wrenn poured his heart, time, and wisdom into shaping his players' lives, guiding them with a dedication that went far beyond the game.

Yet, this unwavering commitment had its price, a hidden tax that only became fully apparent at his funeral. His son, standing amid those who revered Coach Wrenn, shared a poignant, bitter truth. He had grown up sharing his father with hundreds of others, feeling the pain of a personal relationship diluted by his father's expansive role. This revelation sheds light on a rarely discussed aspect of leadership – the personal sacrifices made in the pursuit of guiding others.

Life, in any capacity, is a balancing act of competing identities: the person at home and the person in charge. Every day, leaders are faced with tough choices and decisions that shape not only their professional journey but also the intimate contours of their personal lives. This constant juggling act can be isolating, a silent struggle often overlooked or unacknowledged.

The truth is leaders are human, too. They harbor feelings, face vulnerabilities, and often have a profound desire to connect, particularly because of these sharp, painful dilemmas. The seat of leadership, though elevated, can be a solitary place, marked by internal conflicts and unvoiced yearnings for understanding and camaraderie.

It Is What It Is . . . What If It's Not?

I love thinking about what would happen if we got this all wrong. What if what we think we know and what we have been taught is just not true?

Here are some fun facts we humans got wrong:

- **The earth is not the center of the universe:** For centuries, the geocentric model, which placed the earth at the center of the universe, was an unchallenged truth. This belief was upended by Copernicus, Galileo, and others, who proposed and substantiated the heliocentric model, where the sun, not the earth, is the center of our solar system.
- **Flat earth to round earth:** The idea that the earth was flat was a widely held belief in many ancient cultures. It was later established that the earth is round, a realization that dramatically changed navigation and our understanding of the cosmos.

- **Static universe to expanding universe:** The concept of a static, unchanging universe was prevalent until the 20th century. Edwin Hubble's observations led to the revolutionary idea that the universe is expanding, fundamentally altering our understanding of the cosmos.

- **Newtonian physics to quantum mechanics and relativity:** Newton's laws of motion and universal gravitation were considered the pillars of physics until the 20th century. The emergence of Einstein's theory of relativity and the field of quantum mechanics introduced concepts that were radically different from the Newtonian framework, reshaping our understanding of time, space, and matter.

- **The indestructibility of the atom:** The atom was once thought to be the smallest, indivisible component of matter. Discoveries in atomic physics, particularly the identification of subatomic particles like protons, neutrons, and electrons, debunked this notion.

- **Dietary fats and health:** For decades, dietary fats were vilified as the primary cause of obesity and heart disease. Recent research has a very different view, showing certain types of fats are essential and beneficial for health.

- **Pluto's planetary status:** Once considered the ninth planet of our solar system, Pluto was reclassified as a "dwarf planet" in 2006, changing the way we categorize and understand our solar system.

The Biggest Software Update Ever: How Did All of This Happen?

One of my favorite things to think about is what we don't know but should in order to move forward as a people. To get there, you have to look at the edges, the voices that don't fit the conventional norm.

A renowned author and investigator, Graham Hancock, challenges conventional historical narratives with his in-depth research.[3] Hancock proposes that advanced civilizations, much older than those currently known, existed and thrived thousands of years before our recorded history. His work, based on extensive archaeological, astronomical, and geological studies, suggests these civilizations had access to sophisticated knowledge and technologies.

He theorizes this civilization met its demise due to a catastrophic event during the Younger Dryas period. According to Hancock, the remnants of this society embarked on global voyages, imparting their knowledge of agriculture, monumental architecture, and astronomy to the hunter-gatherer communities they encountered.

He examines megalithic structures around the world, from Gobekli Tepe in Turkey to the pyramids of Egypt, proposing these could be remnants of these lost civilizations. His analysis of astronomical alignments and symbology in these structures suggests a deep understanding of celestial events, far surpassing the expected capabilities of their time.

In books like *Fingerprints of the Gods* and *Magicians of the Gods*, Hancock explores evidence of ancient global cataclysms, proposing that a major event about 12,000 years ago caused a significant setback to human civilization. He points to geological evidence of rapid climate change and mass extinctions that align with this timeline, suggesting the survivors of these advanced civilizations could have passed on their knowledge to hunter-gatherer societies, thus kickstarting what we know as recorded history.

Hancock's work also dives into the realm of altered states of consciousness in ancient rituals. He theorizes psychoactive substances played a significant role in the religious and spiritual practices of these civilizations, contributing to their deep understanding of the human psyche and the universe.

What if we were not the first evolved humans?

Why Stop There? Bridging the Cosmic Gap

In our quest to understand the mysteries of our past and present, one question has increasingly captivated public imagination and scientific inquiry alike: are we alone in the universe?

This profound contemplation has gained unprecedented momentum, particularly in the wake of a groundbreaking report by the *New York Times* in 2017.[4]

These revelations not only captured global attention but also reignited a scientific and philosophical debate about the existence of extraterrestrial life. The significance of this moment in our modern history cannot be overstated.

For centuries, the possibility of nonhuman life forms in the cosmos has been a subject of speculation, myth, and science fiction. However, the emergence of credible reports and the serious attention given to them by a national newspaper marked a shift in the conversation. The answers to this age-old question might indeed be within our grasp, potentially lying in the unexplored frontiers of space and our understanding of it.

Are We Truly Alone?

Encounters: Experiences with Nonhuman Intelligences by Diane Pasulka, a professor of religious studies, brings a scholarly perspective to the discussion of nonhuman life forms and UFO phenomena.[5] Her work combines religious history, technology studies, and contemporary reports of UFO encounters to challenge our perception of reality and our place in the universe.

Pasulka examines how advancements in technology, especially in aerospace and artificial intelligence, are blurring the lines between science fiction and reality. She explores the cultural and religious implications of potential contact with extraterrestrial beings, considering how such an encounter could fundamentally alter our understanding of existence and spirituality.

Drawing on her research and interviews with scientists, government officials, and experiencers of UFO phenomena, Pasulka provides a nuanced exploration of the possibility that we are not alone in the universe. Her work invites readers to consider the implications of such discoveries, not just in terms of extraterrestrial life but also in terms of how we understand consciousness, reality, and the unknown.

For me, these seem like much more interesting discussions than who's going to win the next Superbowl, what the latest reality star is up to, or whatever else is distracting us from ourselves.

Rethinking the Current Moment

By far, two of the most interesting people I spoke to for this book were visionaries Daniel Schmachtenberger and Charles Eisenstein. Both bring unique perspectives on the interconnectedness of life and the future of our societal systems.

Schmachtenberger, with his background in systemic thinking, emphasizes the intricate links between the health of our societal systems and the well-being of the planet. He advocates for a holistic approach to solving global challenges, recognizing every action has far-reaching effects across time and space.

Eisenstein, a philosopher and author, challenges the traditional narratives of competition and materialism. He calls for a shift toward systems that prioritize collective well-being and environmental sustainability. Eisenstein's vision is for a society where prosperity is redefined in terms of relationships, community health, and harmony with nature.

Together, their insights offer a transformative view of our current societal challenges. They propose a future where humanity thrives not through dominance and consumption but through cooperation, empathy, and a deep respect for all life forms. Their dialogues inspire a reimagining of our societal structures, emphasizing the need for a profound shift in our collective values and goals.

In summary, "It is what it is . . . what if it's not?" is not just a question but an invitation to embark on a profound intellectual and spiritual journey. It challenges us to look beyond the established norms, to question, and to open our minds to the endless possibilities of human understanding and existence.

Redefining Success

The chase for more – more money, more power, more fame – has long been seen as a measure of success. However, this narrow definition is expanding to include metrics such as personal fulfillment, happiness, and positive social impact.

Success is increasingly viewed in terms of living a balanced and meaningful life, where achievements in personal growth, relationships, and contributions to society are as important as professional and financial accomplishments.

What are we doing here, folks?

What Say You?

1. **Evolving perspectives:** Think back to a moment when you significantly changed your point of view on an important issue. What prompted this change? How did the process of evolving your perspective influence your understanding of empathy and open-mindedness in both personal interactions and business practices?

2. **It's just business:** Recall an instance where you encountered the phrase "It's just business." How did it affect you or the situation? Did it conflict with your personal values?

3. **Digital detox:** Reflect on your habits regarding the use of devices, screens, and social media. How often do you intentionally disconnect? Explore the impact of these breaks on your well-being and creativity. This prompt encourages a deeper understanding of the balance between connectivity and solitude, highlighting the book's theme of mindfulness in the digital age and its importance for holistic well-being.

Chapter 7

Who Doesn't Love an Underdog?

"Always take the high road."

— Jim Mechlinski

Part 1: In the Room Where It Happened

It was an ordinary day until a voicemail shattered the silence.

"Joe Mechlinski, this is Roger Wrenn."

The voice from the past belonged to a figure who had not crossed my path in over a decade. I had a feeling something was off.

Roger Wrenn wasn't just any coach. He was a legend in Maryland sports, a mastermind in both baseball and football, and he was celebrated for his record-breaking feats. His gift was turning adversity into victory, especially at Patterson High School, a place fraught with challenges and turmoil.

This story, however, delves deeper than Wrenn's sporting accolades. It's about the battleground of Patterson, where each day was a struggle for survival. Wrenn didn't just excel here; he transformed lives amidst this chaos.

To me, he was a mentor and a guiding force, and for many, he was a father figure. He brought tough love that many of us needed, yet he did it with empathy and understanding. He was disciplined and he held the line. Never giving up, but always showing up.

One of my favorite things about him is how he started every football season – the exact same way, "Hello, my name is Roger Wrenn, and I have been preparing for this moment my whole life."

He would put it all out there, saying that nothing will ever stand in the way of him showing up. His commitment transcended mere responsibility as a coach; it was both his duty and his honor.

Before I called him back, memories of Coach Wrenn flooded in. Like the first time he yelled at me to "go around the backstop," a common phrase used when we missed something, and if one of us missed, we all ran.

And the TV interview we did together. We rode in his old car, mostly in silence, aside from the occasional advice not to be nervous. Of course, he was the reason I was nervous because I didn't want to let him down.

Coach Wrenn would often cite my class, the 1994 season, as his most special and prolific. Our little troubled school was ranked number one preseason for the state of Maryland. Based on our previous seasons, Division 1 prospects, and other accolades, it was palpable this was going to be a special season.

Our defensive game was scary good. We had seven shutouts that year, tying a state record. The *Baltimore Sun* frequently highlighted our formidable defense, noting that our opponents avoided running the ball up the middle, a testament to my presence on the field.

And our offense was stacked. In our first playoff game, Willie McGirt, our quarterback, ran for 1,000+ yards and threw for 1,000+ yards in our complicated run-and-shoot offense. The offensive line was led by me at the center, two guards to the left and right who were both 6'4", 280 lbs., and our running back, Ryan Lewis, who was a standout all-star player as well. Willie, Ryan, Tyrone, and I were all named first-team, all-state.

Our second playoff game was against a team called Highpoint, where, ironically, Coach Wrenn attended as a youth. With running backs all over 250 lbs., and a nose guard on me at center who was 6'5", 300 lbs., this school was ranked as one of the biggest teams in the country.

We beat them, but they beat us up. Many of us were hurt heading into the next game against a pretty good school in North County that dressed more than 70 and were anything but unimpressive.

The entire game was close, and we had just scored with 90 seconds left to take the lead. The stadium erupted, and it felt like a huge win was before us.

We kicked off to them and made the mistake of taking out our starters (because most of us went both ways), a decision that would haunt Coach Wrenn for the rest of his career. Our opponent's running back ran it back to score, regain the lead, and win the game.

It was a devastating blow. We all knew we were within inches of winning the championship, an opportunity to change the collective stars of Patterson High School and the student body within it. Sadly, a *w* just wasn't in the cards that day.

To this day, when our teammates see one another, this is inevitably the first thing that comes up. We shared so much together on and off the field – intense life moments, and sometimes death moments. It was a brotherhood then and still is today.

Dialing his number, I braced myself for news. Coach Wrenn in his typical direct fashion said, "Joe, sorry to lay this on you, but I'm dying."

The words hit me like a punch in the gut. Wrenn revealed his battle with a rare form of blood cancer, a fight he'd been quietly enduring for years. Despite the tragic news, there was a calm acceptance in his voice, a testament to a life fully and meaningfully lived.

He said, "Joe, I lived a great life. I have little to complain about."

He asked me to speak at an upcoming event honoring his lifetime achievements. Not about glorifying his successes, he wanted me to share the impact he had on my life. The ever-present teacher, Coach Wrenn always focused the attention on others.

Preparing to honor such a monumental figure was daunting. How could I encapsulate a lifetime of lessons, victories, and transformative moments in a single speech? How could I accurately express the magnitude of impact he had on so many people's lives?

Before we hung up, he said, "I think it's also time I shared how you got into Hopkins. Have you ever wondered?" It turns out that it wasn't a simple tale of academic achievement; it was a collective effort of people in the community.

Hopkins athletic director Bob Scott was a Baltimore City boy and he loved underdogs and would take on the challenge of getting them into Hopkins even though it was often difficult to meet the rigorous academic standards of the admissions office.

The late head football coach Jim Margraff was a man who devoted his life to helping boys become men. Using football as the means and the school as the ends, he prepared us for life and beyond. He would later become the all-time football coach with the most wins both in Hopkins history and in the division as well.

My dad's boss, Joe Cowan, played an interesting role in our family from the first moment he met my father. Forty-seven years ago, my dad walked into Joe's office looking for work and said, "No one will ever work harder for you." Joe's reply? "Go home and tell your wife that everything will be okay."

Coach Wrenn, Coach Margraff, Bob Scott, and Joe Cowan all recognized the potential upside in a young kid from Baltimore City going to Hopkins. They knew it was a golden ticket.

They saw beyond the statistics, recognized my potential, and never wanted me to feel like I didn't belong. All of these men came together with the mentality of, "who says this kid can't make it through one of the country's top 10 schools in the nation from one of the worst schools in Baltimore City?"

This revelation was profound, a realization of the many hands that had quietly guided and shaped my path. It reminded me of what my friend, Jayson Gaignard says, "None of us are self-made; we are all community-made."

I had a feeling, of course, that there was more than just luck that got me into the school. Thankfully, there were forces at play that allowed the door of opportunity to swing open.

This story was more than Wrenn's belief in me; it was a tribute to my father, the unsung hero of my journey. Wrenn saw in me the

Who Doesn't Love an Underdog?

values and strength my father had instilled, which became the foundation of my life.

As I prepared to speak at Wrenn's event, I reflected on his grueling practices, heartfelt talks, and the victories snatched from defeat. His teachings were applicable on the field and off the field – life lessons in perseverance, integrity, and resilience. A unique leadership style that wasn't focused solely on winning, but on building character and nurturing the underdog spirit. He taught us to face challenges head-on, to find strength in adversity, and to always walk in integrity.

His sacred phrases were etched into my memory, like at the start of every football season and his famous line, "Are you hurt or are you injured?" His legacy is a testament to the power of authentic leadership, the kind that shapes not just athletes but also individuals to face the world.

Coach Wrenn's influence on me, and many others is a reminder of the profound impact one person can have when they lead with heart, vision, and an unwavering commitment to the growth of those they mentor.

More than a tribute to a great coach, my speech was an acknowledgment of the power of community, of the collective efforts that lift individuals to heights they never imagined possible. It was a celebration of a man who embodied the true essence of authentic leadership, who saw potential where others saw limitations, and who dedicated his life to turning underdogs into champions, both in sports and in life.

Part 2: Will It Take a Miracle?

In the 1980 Winter Olympics, the US hockey team, composed mainly of college players, achieved one of the most remarkable upsets in Olympic history. Defeating the four-time gold-medal-winning Soviet team, known as the best in the world, they won 4-3 in a thrilling match in Lake Placid, New York. This victory came despite the Soviets having dominated Olympic hockey since 1964 and beating the US team 10-3 in a pre-Olympics exhibition game.

The US team, with an average age of just 22, entered the Olympics as the seventh seed and progressed undefeated through the first round. They faced the top-seeded Soviets in a sold-out match, where the teams were tied 2-2 at the end of the first period. Despite the Soviet's lead in the second period and their domination in gameplay, the US team managed to tie the game in the third period. Mike Eruzione then scored, giving the US team the lead, which they maintained for a historic win, later known as the *miracle on ice*.

More than an Olympic upset, this victory symbolized ideological triumph during the Cold War and brought Americans a sense of pride and celebration during economic and international strife. The US team's win, later celebrated in the 2004 film *Miracle*, was a product of exceptional training, adoption of Soviet passing techniques, and a resilient, rough playing style.

This underdog story remains a remarkable moment in sports history.

What Say You?

Who are your top five favorite underdogs and why?

1.

2.

3.

4.

5.

"There are only two ways to live your life. One is as though nothing is a miracle. The other is as though everything is a miracle."

— *Albert Einstein*

Our fascination with underdogs isn't just a penchant for feel-good stories; it's a reflection of our intrinsic yearning for justice, for witnessing the triumph of tenacity and spirit over the seemingly insurmountable.

The tales of Rudy, Rocky, Ruby Bridges, and Rosa Parks aren't just stories; they are testaments to the power of resilience, courage, and the indomitable human spirit that resonates deeply within us all. These stories inspire because they embody the journey from adversity to achievement, showcasing that, against all odds, following one's heart can indeed alter the course of history. Our admiration of the underdog reveals our love for the hero's journey and the invisible forces that conspire against the potential we might overlook.

Our affinity for underdogs is complex, rooted in a mix of schadenfreude, a desire for a just world, and expectation management. We find a guilty pleasure in the downfall of the mighty, driven by a yearning for fairness and equity. Our emotional investment in the unforeseen triumph highlights our preference for narratives that disrupt the predictable flow of events. Our emotions connect to a deeper societal inclination that longs for balance and justice over power and privilege.

However, the most profound obstacle to recognizing underdog potential, and seeing beyond the conventional, lies in our vested interests, legacy thinking, and cognitive biases.

The past, we assume, dictates the future, anchoring us to what we know and obscuring those who exist beyond the margins of our preconceived notions. This underestimation is certainly an oversight and also a systematic failure to recognize and nurture the seeds of greatness, albeit in unconventional soil.

It's said (but not verified) that Upton Sinclair said, "it's hard to get a man to understand something when his salary depends on his not understanding it."[1] This raises the question: how do our interests blind us to the potential of the underdog?

In confronting these challenges, perhaps the solution isn't to fight our nature but to understand and embrace it as part of our reality. This acceptance doesn't mean complacency; rather, it's an acknowledgment that true change requires a shift not just in mindset but in action.

The world craves authenticity – individuals who walk their talk, embodying courage and resilience. Embracing the underdog within us and recognizing it in others is an act of defiance against conventional wisdom and it's a commitment to creating a world where success is not predefined by one's starting point, but by their journey and authenticity of their path.

This reimagined view aligns with the core message of this book: challenging the status quo, valuing authenticity over conformity, and recognizing true leadership and success are born from embracing and uplifting the underdog.

It's a call to action and a reminder that innovation, progress, and genuine leadership emerge not from the well-trodden path but from the courage to forge new ones.

Daryl Davis and the KKK

Meeting Daryl Davis was one of those moments I'll never forget. In addition to being a musician who jammed with Chuck Berry, Daryl decided to dive headfirst into understanding members of the Ku Klux Klan, as a black man. Yeah, you heard that right. And not by standing at a distance, but by getting right into the thick of it – befriending them, of all things.

At a business event, MasterMindTalks, hosted by Gaignard, I sat down with Darryl. I'll be honest, I had no clue who he was before that day. As he told his story, I was hooked.

His story illustrated the power of curiosity over conflict. He shares that he didn't approach the KKK members with preconceived notions or judgments. Daryl wanted to understand how someone could hate him without knowing him. Kind of mind-blowing when you really think about it.

In his search for truth, he struck up a friendship with Roger Kelly, an Imperial Wizard, which is just a fancy title for a leadership position within the KKK. They'd have conversations over meals at each other's homes. Listening more than he talked, Daryl's approach was kind, understanding, and most of all patient.

Eventually, this approach led to something incredible. Kelly, and more than 200 other members, decided to leave the Klan, handing over their robes to Daryl as a symbol of their transformation.

As he shared his story, I couldn't help but wonder about the echo chambers we're all living in. It's easy to stay comfortable, surrounded by people who only reinforce our existing beliefs. But here's Darryl, stepping way outside his safety zone, challenging his own preconceived notions, and, more important, challenging the perceptions of those who outright hated him.

It makes you think, doesn't it? Change is tough, no doubt about it.

But if Darryl can sit down with members of the KKK and find common ground, surely we can make an effort to understand those who might just seem a little different from us. His story is a giant testament to how active listening, curiosity, and understanding can be powerful enough to change hearts and minds.

And that's what this is all about, isn't it? Stepping out of our comfort zones, confronting our biases, and trying to see the world from someone else's perspective.

If Darryl's story teaches us anything, it's that the most profound changes often start with a simple conversation. So, why not start talking?

A Decade for Underdogs: The 2030 Vision

As we look toward the horizon of 2030, the spirit of the underdog is more relevant than ever. In a world increasingly shaped by rapid technological advancements, environmental challenges, and shifting societal norms, the stories of resilience, innovation, and triumph are not confined to a single year but span the entire decade.

The potential for countries, companies, individuals, and concepts to defy expectations and shape our future is immense. The next transformative success story, one that reshapes our global consciousness, is likely unfolding as we speak.

Embracing the Unexpected: A Future Crafted by Underdogs

Although I don't possess a crystal ball, the trends and patterns emerging on the horizon paint a compelling picture of the future. As we cast our gaze toward 2030, envisioning a world shaped by the resilience and innovation of the underdog, here's a glimpse of what we might expect:

- **Majority over the vocal minority: Redefining democracy and engagement**

    The call for a more inclusive, direct form of democracy will be louder in the 2030s. Inspired by pioneers like Audrey Tang, we envision a future where digital platforms and artificial intelligence (AI)-driven tools democratize the decision-making process, enabling collective intelligence to flourish. This decade sees a shift toward continuous, real-time engagement between leaders and communities, breaking away from outdated feedback mechanisms.

- **Less beats more: The rise of the less is more economy**

  The narrative about growth at all costs flips significantly. The Ozempic economy symbolizes a broader societal shift toward valuing less consumption and more meaningful engagements. Businesses and individuals alike adopt a minimalist approach, focusing on sustainability and quality over quantity. This shift is not just a trend but a fundamental change in how we perceive success and fulfillment. Look for AI to be the big unlock here.

- **More human, not less: The four-day work week becomes standard**

  The transformation of the workplace accelerates with the four-day workweek becoming a global standard by 2030. Companies across the spectrum, from tech giants to small enterprises, embrace this model, recognizing its benefits for productivity, employee well-being, and environmental sustainability. This paradigm shift in work culture reflects a deeper understanding of work-life harmony.

- **Humans beat time: Humanity's embrace of lifelong contribution**

  The concept of retirement undergoes a radical transformation. With advancements in health care extending lifespans, the idea of ceasing to contribute at a certain age becomes outdated. The global gig economy offers opportunities for continued engagement, allowing experienced professionals to share their wisdom while maintaining flexibility. The rise of unretirement highlights the value of experience in a fast-paced, ever-evolving world.

- **Mindful > mind full: A mental health renaissance**

    Psychedelic therapy emerges from the fringes to mainstream acceptance as a powerful tool for mental health treatment. Forward-thinking companies integrate these therapies into their health benefits, recognizing the profound impact on employee well-being. The broader acceptance of psychedelic therapy signals a shift toward holistic approaches to mental health, challenging the dominance of traditional pharmaceutical interventions.

- **Morality > money: AI as humanity's mirror**

    The 2030s frame AI not just as a technological tool but as a reflection of our collective humanity. The development and implementation of AI pose ethical, societal, and existential questions, urging us to confront the core of our values and aspirations. This decade is defined by our response to AI's mirror: whether we use it to advance our highest ideals or let it amplify our deepest flaws.

- **Work to live or live to work? Redefining success and well-being**

    The definition of success undergoes a profound shift, moving away from material accumulation toward a more holistic view that includes mental health, relationships, and personal fulfillment. Society recognizes the importance of emotional openness, especially among men, and the invaluable contributions beyond financial providing. The decade champions a more nuanced understanding of success, one that celebrates well-being and meaningful connections.

163

In the vision of a transformative 2030, I draw inspiration from the forethought and pioneering ideas of these celebrated futurists:

- Buckminster Fuller, with his comprehensive perspective on global sustainability and innovation, foresaw the need for a world that works for all, emphasizing the importance of resource efficiency and environmental stewardship. His concept of "doing more with less" presciently aligns with the emerging less is more economy, highlighting a societal pivot toward minimalism and sustainability.

- Marshall McLuhan's insightful proclamation that "the medium is the message" highlights the profound impact of digital platforms and AI in redefining democracy and engagement. His understanding of the electronic age as a global village is manifested in the 2030s through technology-driven collective intelligence and a democratized decision-making process.

- Alvin Toffler, in his exploration of the Third Wave, anticipated the seismic shift from industrial to information-based societies, predicting the rise of the gig economy and the transformation of the workplace. His vision resonates in the widespread adoption of the four-day workweek and the redefinition of retirement, marking a significant evolution in how we view work and contribution.

- Peter Diamandis, with his optimistic outlook on technology's potential to address global challenges, reflects the era's embrace of AI as humanity's mirror. His advocacy for leveraging exponential technologies to solve humanity's grand challenges is seen in the use of AI to enhance mental health treatment and to foster a more nuanced understanding of success and well-being.

Together, these futurists have laid the groundwork for a 2030 vision that is not only achievable but also already unfolding. Their insights into technology, society, and human potential guide us as we navigate the complexities of the coming decade, ensuring the spirit of the underdog, armed with innovation and resilience, will indeed shape our collective future.

My Long-Term, Underdog Vision for the Workplace in 2030

The year is 2030. Kylie and Zoie awake gently to the soothing sounds of ocean waves, as their smart home eases them into the new day. After a nourishing breakfast and brisk walk with their dogs, they settle into their sleek home office, glancing at the blank tabletop that soon materializes into a vast holographic workspace.

"Good morning, Kylie and Zoie," chimes their AI assistant Jojo warmly. "Welcome back." Today, Jojo represents the symbiotic relationship between human creativity and machine intelligence that has come to define modern business.

As mini holograms pop up showing the faces of their global team members, Kylie and Zoie beam at the sight of their close friends and collaborators. Each person shares a few words on how they feel that morning, synchronizing the collective energy before diving into the day's challenges.

Their workspace fluidly adapts to their needs and desires. As Kylie dives into crafting a key presentation, the environment transforms around her into a creativity cocoon, helping her concentrate. Meanwhile, Zoie vocalizes her evolving ideas to an attentive Jojo, who analyzes and integrates her ideas with insights gathered across the company's consciousness.

When a complex new project comes in, demanding creative solutions, Kylie and Zoie enthusiastically facilitate an animated brainstorm with their team. Human ingenuity and AI's computational power work symbiotically to design optimized proposals. By noon, thrilled by a burst of progress, they zip over on a hyperloop train to Baltimore for an annual all-hands company meeting.

Their CEO highlights core metrics: human happiness indices, ecological regeneration rates, along with profits. She traces their evolution from a company focused purely on profits decades ago into one committed to empowering the self-actualization of every employee today in 2030.

As Kylie and Zoie look into the inspired faces of their colleagues, they feel deeply proud of cocreating this worker paradise, one founded on the principles of radical collaboration, technological augmentation, and ruthless compassion. Their company offers but one glimpse into the future of work in 2030, where AI liberates and amplifies our humanity, while business focuses on nourishing collective well-being on a thriving planet.

The day continues with an immersive ideation session where employees across the globe come together through telepresence robotics and VR to brainstorm innovations of the future. Ideas spill out wildly, encouraged without judgment, as AI assistants analyze correlations and patterns in real-time, visualizing connections.

A young intern in Mexico City proposes drones that polymorphically transform pollution into harmless particulates. A senior engineer examines blending this with swarm robotics for scalable green tech. As concepts ping-pong dynamically, Jojo guides the ideation by highlighting precedents and test cases to ground the visions.

By mid-afternoon, charged with creativity, Kylie decompresses through an alternate reality forest bathing session that transports her into a lush jungle, while Zoie chooses to channel her energy into glass-blowing, facilitated by a haptic robot arm. Both find themselves slipping into near meditative flow states, as work and play fuse together.

They decide to wrap up early to enjoy the outdoors. Tucked into a self-driving car, they gaze and admire the cityscape gliding by – solar-paneled roads power automated traffic flows, while verdant vertical farms and carbon-absorbing buildings dot the landscape.

Alighting at a bustling public square, they're greeted by a kinetic sculpture morphing gracefully with wind patterns. Looking around, they spot several employees mingling joyfully after work, bonding over games, art, and dancing, witnessing connections thriving amidst artful infrastructure centered on ecological harmony and upliftment.

As a glorious sunset casts golden light across the vibrant square, Kylie and Zoie decide to unwind at a new molecular gastronomy restaurant featuring AI-designed menus for optimal nutrition and taste. They laugh over fond memories of surviving on frozen meals and late-night takeout during the grueling early days leading up to their company's transformation.

Over refreshing cocktails personalized to match their biometrics, Kylie pulls up a hologram retrospective showcasing photos and videos across the years. They marvel at the young, hungry entrepreneurs they once were, relentlessly pitching their vision of integrating ethics and purpose into profit-seeking mechanisms before it became trendy.

"We were such underdogs trying to overhaul toxic startup bro culture!" Zoie says. They reminisce over rallying thousands into mass meditation circles, guerrilla planting gardens across the city, and hijacking billboards to spread messages of sustainability.

"It's wild to think some called us militant idealists," Kylie laughs. "But it planted seeds for today." They clink glasses, nostalgic for the exhilarating sense of rebellion around building their company's foundation, even amidst the burnout and despair when it seemed their efforts were in vain.

On their way home, feeling connected to their roots, they pause by a kinetic sculpture from an early artist-in-residence. Attached is a

Who Doesn't Love an Underdog?

plaque thanking the trailblazers who paved the way for the cultural renaissance the city now enjoys.

Kylie and Zoie read the dedication, overcome with humility and pride in what emerged from their resilient belief in doing business differently back in 2024.

They stand in silence amidst the whooshing sculpture, watching how its swirling plastic parts catch the moonlight. Once destined for landfills, now transformed into art that delights the public, it reminds them of their company's emergence from struggle into success. Their vision sprouted this small seed that grew roots underground before blossoming years later into a tree offering shade and comfort for generations to come.

Complicated Conversations

As we draw this chapter on leadership to a close, I want to revisit a pivotal moment that predated the global upheaval of the pandemic: the "Complicated Conversations" event I hosted in 2019 in my home-town of Baltimore.

This gathering, an assembling of some of the biggest and bright-est minds, was a deep dive into the realms of mortality and morality, themes that would soon become the crucible within which global consciousness was tested and transformed. It was an initiation into a period of profound introspection and a reevaluation of the values that underpin our collective and individual journeys.

Headliners included Richard Saul Wurman (founder of TED), Steve Kottler (*New York Times* bestselling author and founder of Flow Research Collective), Chris Wilson (*New York Times* bestselling author and artist), and Lola Manekin (founder of Tribe).

An embodiment of the resilience of the human spirit and its capacity for growth, this event served as a reminder that at the edge of what we know lies the opportunity for profound transformation.

It underscored the essence of *Who Says?* – the valor in questioning, the power of challenging entrenched norms, and the vital necessity of stepping into the discomfort of the unknown to uncover new paths of innovation and progress.

The ethos of SHIFT, and indeed the core message of this book, champions the courage to engage in these necessary yet challenging conversations. It's a recognition of the bravery required not only to confront the unknown but also to embrace it, to admit the limits of our understanding, and to commit to a dialogue that seeks deeper understanding and growth.

The pre-pandemic discussions on mortality and morality were in a way prophetic, setting the stage for introspective dialogue that would prove to be indispensable while navigating the complexities of a soon-to-be rapidly changing world. In essence, *Who Says?* and the leadership philosophy it advocates, is a homage to those willing to embrace the underdog spirit.

It's a call to action for each of us to question more deeply, to listen more intently, and to engage in the complicated conversations that challenge us to grow beyond our perceived limits. It invites us to see leadership not as a position of power but as a journey of authentic engagement with the world, where success is measured not by the attainment of personal goals but by the impact of our actions on the collective well-being.

As we move forward, carry lessons from your own critical conversations and an understanding that our greatest advances lie in our willingness to confront the uncomfortable, to embrace the unknown, and to lead with a spirit of curiosity and compassion.

The future belongs to those who are brave enough to believe that within every challenge lies the seed of opportunity, and true leadership is born from the courage to nurture these seeds into pathways of change and transformation.

What Say You?

1. **Reflecting on resilience:** Think of a time when you, like an underdog, overcame significant challenges or adversity. What strengths did you discover in yourself during this time, and how have these experiences shaped your approach to present-day challenges?

2. **The power of mentorship:** Coach Wrenn played a pivotal role in shaping lives through his guidance and mentorship. Reflect on a mentor who has significantly affected your life. What lessons did they impart, and how have you applied these lessons in your personal or professional journey? **Bonus:** if you haven't thanked them, reach out and share what their mentorship meant to you.

3. **Embracing the underdog within:** Considering the stories of resilience and triumph shared in the chapter, how can you embrace the underdog spirit in your own life? What challenges or societal norms do you feel compelled to challenge, and what first step can you take toward making a difference?

4. **The role of community:** The chapter highlights the importance of community support in achieving seemingly impossible goals. Reflect on how your community or support network has influenced your growth and opportunities. How can you contribute to creating a supportive environment for others who may feel like underdogs in their own right?

5. **Identify a current challenge where you feel like an underdog. What steps can you take to turn this challenge into an opportunity?**

Chapter 8

The Awakening: An Invitation for Self-Actualization

"The only way out, is through."

— Robert Frost

Part 1: Coming Home

"You're right where you need to be. We're here for you if you need anything. You're about to take the ride you've always wanted to take."

Our guide handed each of us a capsule, loaded with a dose of psychedelic medicine that was based on our own individual needs.

Lying on the cabin floor with four other people in what they call a "squish room" on top of foam mattresses and pillows, I had a gravity blanket of 25 to 30 pounds draped across my body. With a blindfold blocking out all light and noise-canceling headphones, I lay back listening to the soothing music. The guide's voice comes softly into my headphones as if he were inside of my head.

"You're going to take three long breaths in and then three breaths out to a count of eight." We take the three long breaths in and then three long breaths out. "And now, on the last breath, instead of breathing out, I want you to hold it in for as long as you can."

My heart rate begins to slow down as my anxieties, concerns, and needs all melt away. Relaxing fully into being, that which needs nothing and never has, I experience a level of ease I've never felt before.

The medicine begins to kick in and it feels like we're at the top of a roller coaster.

Click . . . click . . . click . . . almost to the top and about to crest.

Suddenly, a soft rush gently filled my body bringing a feeling of safety and comfort. The gravity blanket is getting heavier and the squishiness under me is getting softer. It felt like I was in a warm cocoon filled with pink and purple hues and a bright light all around me. The feeling of pure love fills my chest.

The image changes and I see a baby, about one year old, being held by a young mother. And then I see the mother crying quietly while the baby is in the corner of a crib.

Once again, the image changes, and I see the baby from another vantage point, through the eyes of something unfamiliar. The more I bring my attention to the baby, the more he recognizes my presence as someone close to him.

In looking at the baby, I realize that I'm looking at this baby through the lens of someone who is not me. A new vantage point, a whole new palette of emotional colors shows up.

I feel my heart swell with immense love and pride. Slowly I realize I am being given the gift of seeing the baby grow through Debbie, my mom's eyes.

Familiar emotions of not having enough and anxiety are present. An immense fear for the baby's well-being fills my body. I can feel how I'm struggling with my own life as a woman in her early twenties. I want to be an actress, on stage, and become a star. I want to be seen and successful. As I look at the baby boy, I'm overwhelmed with a completely new set of emotions. Life feels very hard, like there's a lot of struggle and strife with not many answers to the daily challenges.

The images shift, and I can see the little boy, through the eyes of the mother, tying his shoelaces for the first time. Zooming out beyond the mother and child, I realize this woman loves this baby, loves me, more than any person on the planet. I know deep inside of myself, that we will always be connected.

As I watch this young mother with her little boy, all I can feel is forgiveness and grace as I understand now that our life was perfect in all the ways it needed to be.

A series of snapshot images, one after another, of the little boy growing up seen through her eyes flashed through my consciousness.

As Debbie, I feel that the boy is special and believe he's going to make it. I know he will find a way, no matter what. I feel pride watching how he makes difficult choices at school and tries to the best of his ability to make good decisions.

It's funny because as his mother I don't take any credit for how he grows and develops. I realize I'm just shepherding him on this journey and will be a part of his success as much as I can be.

I see him at preschool standing up for a young girl being harassed by a bunch of boys, and I'm so proud of how he isn't intimidated by the biggest one, even as he gets punched in the face.

I see him make his way through first grade: he becomes a great learner and student. He has a tremendous capacity to absorb knowledge about new things. I see his immense generosity. I see him helping others in all kinds of little and big ways.

I see his first-grade teacher passing out in front of the class, and he's the first one by the teacher's side and then runs to get help. I see how he makes the right decisions for everyone every time the stakes are high.

I see another image of my boy in fifth grade and his teacher blaming another kid Jason for something Joey did, and I see my son courageously raise his hand in front of the class to set the record straight, "It wasn't Jason. It was me; I did it."

As I see more and more quick snapshots of this boy growing up into a young man through the eyes of his mother, I realize deeply that there have been no mistakes.

Everything that had happened in my life began to make sense. Being born to a young mother with diabetes, being under such pressure as a child, growing up to be a young adult who became her caregiver, all the way up to the moments of her death, all blossomed into recognition and acceptance, right in this moment under the gravity blanket.

It's like a movie, and I am the main character. The movie is about the choices I get to make and the way I create even with less than ideal raw materials. I understand now that the purpose of this journey isn't to have an easy ride; it's about what you make of this one life.

I feel tremendous compassion for myself, realizing that the narrative we've all been fed about fitting in to be accepted is wrong. And stepping out of the trance to remember why you're really here, which is to create art, not fit into someone else's agenda.

Shifting under the weight of the gravity blanket, I feel discomfort realizing all of the ways I've contorted myself to withstand the tremendous pressure to make money so that I'm never poor again, and to conform to the rules of the game I've been taught to play.

With a sigh of relief, I accept that none of that is going to work anymore. It can't possibly work, especially at this time when so many of my old ways are falling apart. The old rules cannot and don't apply anymore.

Light and energy fill my chest as I see how every little thing that has happened in my life has been instrumental and indispensable, leading me to sing the song I was born to sing.

My eyes open wide suddenly to find that it's still black under the blindfold.

"What the fuck is my song?" I ask myself, with urgency. "I can faintly get the feeling of it, the flavor of it. But how can I give it words? What is the song I am meant to sing?"

I know now, without any shadow of a doubt, that my unique song is the accumulation of all these experiences, every single one of them. Nothing was irrelevant. How am I going to give that authentic expression?

By teaching what I need to learn and creating what I need to heal.

"I am loving awareness."

— *Spiritual leader Ram Dass*

175

The Awakening

In the realm of personal and professional development, the concept of flow states – where one is fully immersed and operating at their peak – has garnered significant attention. Research by the Flow Research Collective highlights that achieving flow can increase productivity by up to 500%.[1]

This chapter explores how psychedelic therapy, by fostering deep introspection and enhanced mental flexibility, can serve as a catalyst for achieving these coveted states of consciousness, thereby revolutionizing our approach to work and personal fulfillment.

Buckle up.

Part 2: The Depths of Self

Embarking on the path of psychedelic therapy is like setting sail on uncharted waters, where each wave and wind brings you closer to the core of your being. It's a commitment – a pledge to face the entirety of oneself, the shadows as much as the light, with unwavering honesty and courage.

This journey isn't about escaping the reality of our lives but about engaging with it more fully, confronting our deepest fears, traumas, and aspirations.

How Often Do We Dare to Look Within with Such Radical Honesty?

I thought I had a decent practice of this until I realized how easy it is to convince ourselves we're being radically honest only to find we're in our own echo chamber doing our best to avoid discomfort and inconvenient truths.

This path cannot be embarked on lightly because it demands a holistic approach to healing. Psychedelic therapy is but one piece of a larger, intricate puzzle. It's critical to set expectations that are grounded in reality, understanding that this process may surface traumas we've long avoided. Far from a quick fix, this is a journey of deep and sometimes arduous transformation that promises genuine growth and healing.

The bedrock of this transformative expedition lies in creating a solid therapeutic foundation, a feat greatly attributed to the pioneering efforts of the Multidisciplinary Association for Psychedelic Studies (MAPS).

MAPS has been instrumental in championing the cause of psychedelic research and therapy toward a holistic healing approach. Their founder and CEO, Rick Doblin, deserves a mountain of gratitude.

By weaving together elements of talk therapy, mindfulness, physical wellness, and more, he faces head-on the exhaustive process of healing that transcends the bounds of psychedelic sessions alone. The aim is to integrate these profound experiences into our daily existence as we continue the pursuit of healing and personal evolution.

Venturing into the realm of psychedelic therapy mirrors the ethos of *Who Says?* Questioning the established narrative and rules, embracing our authentic selves, and remaining open to new models of understanding and healing. It's a journey of not only healing but also of discovering who we truly are and who we have the potential to become.

As we embark on this journey, let's not overlook the significance of how this is part of a larger dialogue about mental health. By exploring these therapies, we advocate for a more empathetic, compassionate, and holistic approach to mental health and overall well-being.

Reasons for Resistance

There are many reasons people avoid this conversation. Here are a few I hear most often:

- **Fear of stigma:** Although this is dwindling, many people fear the judgment that comes along with exploring unconventional therapies.
- **Misinformation:** A lack of accurate information, or misinformation, fuels misconceptions.
- **Fear of losing control:** The idea of surrendering to the psychedelic experience can be intimidating, especially for those that need to control.
- **Doubts about efficacy:** Skepticism arises from unfamiliarity with the science behind psychedelics.

- **Legal and ethical concerns:** Uncertainty about the legal status of psychedelics and ethical considerations can deter interest.

Sharing my perspective on psychedelic therapy isn't to persuade, but to inform. I hope my personal experience serves as an example for those seeking guidance or clarity.

Whether psychedelic therapy is your path or not, the quest for understanding, healing, and authenticity is a shared journey.

What Say You?

Reflective exercise: Pause to reflect on your inner landscape.

1. What fears or traumas have you sidestepped or avoided?

2. How could confronting this lead to personal empowerment and growth?

Over Consuming and Under Feeling: The Catalyst for Change

A caterpillar voraciously consumes up to 27,000 times its body weight in its journey toward metamorphosis. In our pre-pandemic societal norms, we mirrored a caterpillar.

We lived in a world where the emphasis on accumulation and immediate gratification led us to overlook the consequences of our actions on the environment, our communities, and our mental well-being. COVID-19 thrust us into an unexpected chrysalis of introspection and recalibration.

Within this cocoon of global adversity, we were offered a chance not just to grow but to transform fundamentally. Emerging into a post-pandemic reality, it's clear we cannot return to the unsustainable patterns of the past. The pandemic served as a powerful wake-up call, highlighting the fragility of our existing systems and the urgent need for a shift toward sustainability and mindfulness.

Our transformation, much like the caterpillar's, is about evolving into more conscious beings who understand the importance of balance and harmony with the natural world. This shift is our era's defining challenge, a nudge from Mother Nature herself to find equilibrium after years of excess. This period of collective introspection has also revealed the limitations of traditional approaches to mental wellness. In our quest for productivity and success, we've often neglected the emotional and psychological dimensions of our lives, relying on antiquated methods to address complex mental health issues.

The increasing interest in psychedelic-assisted psychotherapy within the workplace is a testament to a growing recognition that we must explore every avenue to support mental health. This innovative approach, once marginalized, is now being embraced by forward-thinking employers who understand that the well-being of their employees is paramount.

The profound benefits reported by those who have undergone psychedelic-assisted therapy accentuate the need for a more holistic approach to mental health, one that addresses the root causes rather than merely managing symptoms.

The workplace, as a concentrated reflection of society, possesses immense potential to drive change. By prioritizing mental health and embracing unconventional therapies, employers can challenge the status quo and cultivate environments where wellness and growth go hand in hand.

The significance of integrating psychedelic-assisted psychotherapy into health plans extends beyond the immediate impact on individuals. This revolution represents a broader shift toward acknowledging and addressing the mental health crisis facing our society.

With mental health challenges like depression contributing to significant losses in productivity and human potential, the conventional reliance on SSRIs and other traditional treatments has often fallen short. Psychedelic-assisted psychotherapy provides hope and offers a pathway to healing as transformative as the journey from caterpillar to butterfly. It can be a transformation that requires courage, openness, and a willingness to explore the unknown.

The embrace of psychedelic-assisted psychotherapy in the workplace is not just a trend; it's a reflection of a more profound societal shift happening that values mental health and well-being as essential components of a sustainable future. In this journey toward balance and mindfulness, the path to healing and growth lies not only in changing how we work but also in redefining our relationship with ourselves and the world around us.

Reframing Psychedelic Therapy: A Journey from Post-Traumatic Stress Disorder to Post-Traumatic Growth

The impetus behind the embrace of psychedelic therapy is twofold: a deep-seated yearning for healing from psychological scars and an aspiration for a level of consciousness that transcends ordinary existence. My own path through the dark forest of post-traumatic stress disorder (PTSD), shadowed by the ghosts of mortality, the reverberations of six concussions, and the remnants of physical aggression encountered in sports, mirrors a collective struggle.

This struggle permeates through the very fabric of our society, affecting countless lives often relegated to the margins of our collective consciousness. The conversation about PTSD, historically limited to the experiences of combat veterans, expands significantly when we consider the insights of works like Bessel van der Kolk's *The Body Keeps the Score* and the profound reflections of Gabor Maté, prompting a reevaluation of trauma and its pervasive influence.[2]

In a society that prioritizes physical well-being at the expense of mental health, the quest for inner peace and healing often leads to uncharted territories. My pursuit of mindfulness, which began with journaling and gratitude, found a new direction in 2017 through psychedelic therapy. The insights provided by Aldous Huxley in *The Doors of Perception* merely hinted at the possibilities. Still, it was my firsthand experiences with MDMA and psilocybin that ushered in new unlocks of understanding and healing.[3]

This journey was not merely about confronting the shadows cast by trauma but about transcending them, moving toward what is now increasingly recognized as post-traumatic growth (PTG). PTG represents the transformative potential that lies in the aftermath of trauma, a concept that psychedelic therapy uniquely positions itself to facilitate.

Unlike traditional treatments, which often focus on managing symptoms, psychedelic therapy offers a pathway to reframe and integrate traumatic experiences, fostering growth, resilience, and a newfound appreciation for life. This paradigm shift from surviving to thriving encapsulates the essence of PTG, highlighting the capacity for individuals to emerge from the depths of despair with greater strength, wisdom, and a deeper connection to themselves and the world around them.

As we navigate the complexities of mental health and societal well-being, the integration of psychedelic therapy into mainstream health care offers not just a cure but a doorway to rediscovery and growth.

In this light, the journey from PTSD to PTG is not just possible but essential, marking a critical step toward healing both individuals and the collective psyche of our society.

What Say You?

Reflect on a moment when you felt truly understood by someone at work.

What did that experience teach you about the kind of leader you aspire to be?

Journal your thoughts and consider how empathy and understanding can be further integrated into your own leadership style.

It's a Shame to Ignore the Science and Momentum

According to the 2023 National Veteran Suicide Prevention Annual Report released by the Department of Veterans Affairs, 17 veterans, on average, die by suicide each day in the United States.[4]

For every ribbon sticker and every "support our troops" mantra, we must confront the reality: denying veterans and others who have PTSD access to psychedelic-assisted therapy is morally indefensible. In MAPS' groundbreaking Phase 2 trials, 61% of participants no longer qualified for PTSD after just three sessions of MDMA-assisted therapy.[5]

Read that again. The evidence is irrefutable. The results literally speak for themselves. These substances provide a gateway to confronting and processing trauma with a clarity and fearlessness that traditional treatments fail to deliver.

Yet, we find ourselves at a pivotal juncture, hindered by societal stigma and archaic laws that impede our healing journey. The endorsement of harmful substances like alcohol, alongside the demonization of psychedelics – a vestige of the late 1960s counterculture backlash – has deprived us of decades of progress in mental health treatment.

The Controlled Substances Act of 1970, which lumped LSD and psilocybin with the likes of heroin, was not just a legislative misstep – it was a moral failure, one that has stifled research and denied countless individuals the relief they desperately need.

It's Time to Call Out the Hypocrisy

The results are in, the evidence clear, and the path forward illuminated. To continue to outlaw these treatments is to turn our backs on those who've borne the brunt of our collective traumas.

This isn't a drug promotional commercial, but a challenge to the status quo, another way we can seek to ask ourselves, why have these treatments been historically marginalized? Who says we can't use these in a safe and effective way to heal ourselves? We must find the courage to question outdated norms and demand a health care system that truly serves every individual's mental and emotional well-being.

As we push for change, let's remember the stakes. This is more than a debate; it's a battle for the soul of our approach to mental health. The time for half-measures and platitudes is over. It's time for bold action for the sake of every individual who's ever been told to "just get over" their trauma.

Our moral compass must guide us toward compassion, understanding, and above all, access to every tool in our arsenal for healing. The psychedelic renaissance is not just coming; it's here, and it's a fight we cannot afford to lose.

More Data

- **Neuroplasticity enhancement:** Studies, including one published in *Cell Reports* in 2018, demonstrate that psychedelics like psilocybin can significantly increase neuroplasticity, suggesting a mechanism behind the therapeutic effects for mental health conditions.[6]

- **Global decriminalization and legalization efforts:** As of 2021, Oregon became the first US state to legalize psilocybin for therapeutic use, and Denver became the first US city to decriminalize psilocybin in 2019. Internationally, Portugal decriminalized the possession of all drugs in 2001, focusing on treatment over punishment.[7]

- **Traditional use in spiritual and healing practices:** The Eleusinian Mysteries, an ancient Greek rite, are believed to have involved the ingestion of a psychoactive potion, kykeon, as early as 1500 BCE, highlighting the long-standing human relationship with psychedelic substances for spiritual exploration.[8]

- **Improvements in end-of-life anxiety:** A 2016 study published in the *Journal of Psychopharmacology* found a single dose of psilocybin significantly reduced anxiety and depression in cancer patients, with about 80% of participants showing sustained benefits six months after treatment.[9]

- **Microdosing trends:** An observational study published in 2019 in *PLOS One* found participants who practiced microdosing reported improved mood, focus, and creativity, indicating a potential non-traditional use of psychedelics that warrants further research.[10]

- **Economic impact on mental health treatment:** A 2020 analysis by the *Journal of Psychopharmacology* estimated psilocybin therapy could save the US health care system up to $16 billion annually by reducing the costs associated with mental health conditions like depression and PTSD.[11]

- **Psychedelic-assisted psychotherapy training programs:** Institutions like the California Institute of Integral Studies have launched certification programs in psychedelic-assisted therapies, preparing mental health professionals for the integration of these treatments into clinical practices.[12]

- **Impact on creativity and problem-solving:** Historical accounts and anecdotal evidence suggest psychedelics can foster creative breakthroughs. A study in *Psychopharmacology* (2012) found low doses of mescaline significantly enhanced problem-solving abilities, offering potential insights into the cognitive benefits of psychedelics.[13]

For those who are unaware, Johns Hopkins, New York University, the Imperial London of College, and Stanford University have all been researching these substances on and off for decades.

And, if you are new to this conversation, I recommend these reads:

- *The Psychedelic Explorer's Guide: Safe, Therapeutic, and Sacred Journeys* by James Fadiman (Park Street Press, 2011).

  This guide is an indispensable resource for anyone curious about the safe and effective use of psychedelics. Fadiman offers a comprehensive overview of how these substances can be used for therapeutic growth, emphasizing the importance of set and setting, and the profound potential these experiences have for personal transformation.

- *How to Change Your Mind: What the New Science of Psychedelics Teaches Us About Consciousness, Dying, Addiction, Depression, and Transcendence* by Michael Pollan (Penguin Books, 2011)

  Michael Pollan provides an engaging exploration of the renaissance in psychedelic research, blending personal anecdotes with rigorous science to demystify the psychedelic experience. His work makes a compelling case for the therapeutic benefits of psychedelics, inviting readers to reconsider their potential to profoundly alter human consciousness.

- *Stealing Fire: How Silicon Valley, the Navy SEALs, and Maverick Scientists Are Revolutionizing the Way We Live and Work* by Steven Kotler and Jamie Wheal (Dey Street Books, 2017)

  Kotler and Wheal take readers on a thrilling exploration of how elite performers across various domains are harnessing altered states of consciousness to break boundaries and enhance performance. The book explores the use of psychedelics, meditation, and flow states, revealing the cutting-edge science behind achieving peak human potential.

- *The Doors of Perception* by Aldous Huxley (Harper Perennial, 2009)

  Aldous Huxley's seminal work offers a mesmerizing account of his experiences with mescaline, exploring the profound impact of psychedelics on perception and the human experience. Huxley's philosophical reflections provide a foundational perspective on the potential of psychedelics to expand our understanding of reality.

- *A Dose of Hope: A Story of MDMA-Assisted Psychotherapy* by Dr. Dan Engle (Lioncrest Publishing, 2021)

  Dr. Dan Engle talks about the healing potential of MDMA-assisted psychotherapy, combining scientific insights with heart-touching narratives. This book highlights the groundbreaking research and personal stories of healing, underscoring MDMA's promise in the treatment of PTSD and other mental health disorders.

- *LSD and the Mind of the Universe: Diamonds from Heaven* by Christopher M. Bache (Park Street Press, 2019)

  Christopher M. Bache shares his extraordinary journeys through LSD-induced states of consciousness, offering a profound exploration of the spiritual and transformative potential of psychedelics. Bache's narrative challenges readers to consider the deeper cosmic meanings revealed through these experiences.

- *Sacred Knowledge: Psychedelics and Religious Experiences* by William A. Richards (Columbia University Press, 2015)

  William A. Richards explores the intersection of psychedelics and spirituality, presenting a compelling argument for the role of entheogens in eliciting deeply meaningful religious experiences. Richards's insights contribute to the broader understanding of psychedelics as tools for spiritual awakening and personal growth.

- *The Immortality Key: The Secret History of the Religion with No Name* by Brian C. Muraresku (St. Martin's Press, 2020)

  Brian C. Muraresku's investigative work uncovers the hidden history of psychedelic sacraments in early Christian and pre-Christian rituals. Through a meticulous examination of archaeological and textual evidence, he reveals how psychoactive substances shaped religious experiences in the ancient world.

- *The Sacred Mushroom and the Cross: A Study of the Nature and Origins of Christianity Within the Fertility Cults of the Ancient Near East* by John M. Allegro (Dreamscape Media, 2022)

  John M. Allegro's controversial book posits that early Christian rites may have been influenced by ancient fertility cults and psychedelic mushrooms. His provocative thesis offers an alternative perspective on the origins of Christianity, grounded in linguistic analysis and historical research.

- *Food of the Gods: The Search for the Original Tree of Knowledge; A Radical History of Plants, Drugs, and Human Evolution* by Terence McKenna (Tantor Audio, 2012)

  Terence McKenna's captivating narrative suggests that the evolution of human consciousness was significantly influenced by our ancestors' interactions with psychoactive plants. McKenna's work invites readers to reevaluate the role of psychedelics in human history and culture.

Psychedelic Therapy at Work: Widening Your Circle of Concern

In the ever-evolving landscape of corporate wellness, SHIFT has embarked on a pioneering journey to redefine the boundaries of traditional health benefits. We've embraced the groundbreaking realm of ketamine-assisted psychotherapy, not as a novel experiment, but as a testament to our unwavering commitment to the mental health and productivity of our workforce.

Recent research by the World Health Organization found every $1 invested in scaling up treatment for common mental disorders such as depression and anxiety leads to a return of $4 in improved health and productivity.[14] This transformative decision was born out of a recognition of the profound impact such therapies can have, marking a bold leap toward a more compassionate and productive workplace.

The inspiration for this audacious move came from none other than Dr. Bronner, an amazing example of holistic health practices within the corporate sphere. My personal conversation with David Bronner, the CEO of Dr. Bronner's, was nothing short of enlightening.

Hearing the genuine concern in his voice and witnessing his dedication to employee well-being, it became clear this was more than a health benefit – it was a mission to uplift and change lives.

Each year, as employees sifted through their usual health plan options, a groundbreaking alternative emerged – psychedelic drugs. This inclusion, championed by a handful of visionary employers, signifies a seismic shift in our approach to mental wellness at work. It's a bold acknowledgment that the prevailing strategies to combat the mental health crisis, exacerbated by the COVID-19 pandemic, are no longer sufficient.

Psychedelic-assisted therapy, particularly the ketamine-assisted treatments offered by pioneers like Mindbloom, are paving the way. SHIFT's partnership with them is a reflection of our belief that mental health care is a right, not a privilege. These once-marginalized therapies are now recognized for their potential to revolutionize the treatment of depression, anxiety, PTSD, and other mental health challenges.

The decision to incorporate psychedelic-assisted psychotherapy into our health benefits package is underpinned by a wealth of evidence supporting the efficacy of psychedelics in mental health care. From neurogenesis to the unlocking of revolutionary therapeutic insights, substances such as ketamine, MDMA, and psilocybin are reshaping our understanding of healing and treatment.

Ketamine therapy, in particular, has emerged as a frontrunner, lauded for its rapid antidepressant effects by leading researchers like Dr. John Krystal. Despite regulatory and cost barriers, the off-label use of generic ketamine offers a glimmer of hope to those who have found little relief in standard treatments.

By championing psychedelic-assisted psychotherapy, we join a vanguard of employers who understand that the well-being of their workforce is paramount to organizational success. This holistic approach to health benefits not only addresses the symptoms of workplace stress and mental health issues but also unlocks healing, creativity, and engagement. As we move forward, our commitment at SHIFT remains unwavering: to challenge the status quo, advocate for the comprehensive health of our team, and set a precedent in the corporate world.

Psychedelic therapy isn't a universal solution, nor is it a decision to be taken lightly. It's a deeply personal choice and requires an understanding that this form of medicine is not a cure-all or an easy escape from life's pains. Rather, it's a tool – a means to unlock deeper healing and understanding within ourselves, provided we're prepared for the journey ahead.

Considering psychedelic therapy has the potential to surface traumas and emotions we've yet to process, it can be challenging and even painful, but it's where the potential for real healing lies. For those considering this path, know it's just one component of a broader therapeutic practice. True healing comes from a holistic approach that may include talk therapy; mindfulness practices like meditation, physical wellness, sound therapy; and more. The goal is to build a support system and a set of practices that can help you integrate your experiences and continue the work of healing beyond the psychedelic sessions themselves.

I share these insights not as an advocate or even a detractor but as someone who has walked this path and learned from it. As always, the decision is deeply personal, and what's right for one may not be right for another. For me, it was one of the best decisions I've personally made in my own healing.

Flow at Work

Steven Kottler and Rian Doris of the Flow Research Collective are the world's leading experts in flow – a state where one's sense of time dilates, productivity skyrockets, and creativity flourishes. Empirical data curated by the collective indicates individuals in flow can experience up to a 500% boost in productivity, with creativity rates doubling, and learning speeds accelerating dramatically.[15]

The collective's research, grounded in rigorous scientific inquiry, reveals that certain triggers, including challenging tasks that align closely with one's skill level, can reliably induce this coveted state. Moreover, the introduction of psychedelics into this equation marks a frontier of untapped potential. Controlled studies have demonstrated that psychedelics, by facilitating a temporary dissolution of ego and reducing prefrontal cortex activity, can significantly lower the barriers to entering flow states, thus enhancing creativity, problem-solving capabilities, and overall mental flexibility.

"A bad day for the ego is a good day for the soul."
– *Robin Sharm, bestselling author and leadership expert*

Integrating this data into workplace wellness programs could herald a new era of productivity and employee satisfaction. Imagine a workplace where, supported by data-driven strategies from the Flow Research Collective, employees routinely access flow states, leveraging both traditional triggers and, where legally and ethically permissible, psychedelic-assisted methodologies to amplify their natural capabilities.

Such an approach promises to elevate individual and collective performance and create a work environment characterized by unprecedented levels of engagement, satisfaction, and well-being.

As we chart the future of work in *Who Says?*, the synthesis of flow science and psychedelic research offers a compelling blueprint for cultivating high-performance teams equipped to navigate the complexities of the modern world with grace, creativity, and unparalleled efficiency.

More Rabbit Holes? Revealing Hidden Legacies: The Immortality Key

Before you turn the page to the next chapter, there's one more literary rabbit hole to jump into, *The Immortality Key* by Brian C. Muraresku (St. Martin's Press, 2020) (as introduced previously in this chapter). This book uncovers the lost history of psychedelic sacraments in ancient religious rituals. His investigation focuses on the Eucharist, the central rite of Christian worship, proposing that its origins might be traced back to psychedelic practices among early Christians and even further to the Eleusinian Mysteries of ancient Greece.

Muraresku examines archaeological findings, ancient texts, and linguistic patterns to construct a narrative of how psychoactive substances may have been integral to religious experiences. His research highlights the use of ergot, a fungus with psychedelic properties, in the making of the sacred beer and wine consumed during the Eleusinian Mysteries. His research offers a new perspective on the spiritual experiences of Jesus and his disciples.

The book also explores the role of women in these ancient rituals, suggesting they might have been the primary carriers of this psychedelic knowledge. Muraresku's work raises questions about the suppression of female-led religious practices and the subsequent loss of sacred pharmacological knowledge during the rise of patriarchal structures in religion.

That's right, I see this as possibly one of the biggest discoveries of women's rights. Brian's work clearly highlights the role women played which was *not* from the "rib of Adam" and in the second seat.

As we look to the future, the lines between personal growth and professional development continue to blur. Leaders who embrace their own mental health journeys will pave the way for organizations where well-being is woven into the very fabric of their culture.

What Say You?

1. **Reflect on your own journey of self-discovery and healing.** What are the shadows within yourself that you've been reluctant to confront? Write about these hidden aspects and consider what they can teach you about your strengths, vulnerabilities, and the path to greater authenticity

2. **Explore the concept of growth through discomfort.** How have your most challenging experiences contributed to your personal and professional development? Journal about these moments and the lessons they've imparted.

3. **Consider your perspectives on mental health and wellness.** How have these views evolved over time, and what role, if any, do you believe innovative therapies like psychedelic therapy should play in modern health care?

4. **In contemplating the balance between overconsumption and mindfulness, identify areas of your life where**

you could benefit from more intentional living. How can you apply the principles of balance and sustainability to foster a more fulfilling personal and professional life?

5. **Write a letter to a younger version of yourself. What advice and wisdom would you share about facing fears and embracing growth?**

Chapter 9

What Say You?

"If you know the way broadly, you will see it in everything."
— Miyamoto Musashi, a 16th-century Japanese Kensei

Part 1: The Legend of Eddie

"Eddie's gone."

These words are etched in my heart forever.

Every Friday, my dad and I have a tradition. We connect to reflect on the week that just passed and how we crushed it or how it crushed us. However, on the morning of Friday, March 10, 2023, something was different.

At 9:38 a.m., my phone rang, and it was my dad. The early timing caught me off guard. Usually, our check-ins happen at the end of the day, so I instantly sensed something was up.

Losing loved ones is an unavoidable aspect of the human journey, but this one was an emotional earthquake no one saw coming. My brother Eddie, a young 50 at the time of his death, lived a hard life, and life was hard right back.

He was an OG, an old soul, and wise in the ways of life and the streets. The role he played, and the impact he had on my life, were as big as it gets.

As I began writing this book, *Who Says?*, little did I know the influence he and our relationship would wield over its creation. We met when I was 7, and he was 11. I was instantly infatuated with his cooler-than-cool, bigger-than-life, heart-of-a-warrior vibe.

His mom, Rose, and my dad married, which brought us all together. A few years later, our little sister, Marisa, entered the world. It was a blended family, but it never felt that way.

Within five minutes of meeting and playing catch in the alley, he said if anyone messed with me in the neighborhood, to tell them we were brothers and he had my back. What I should have gotten clear on is who was I supposed to call if he was the one messing with me!?

After school and on weekends, I joined the neighborhood crew, running alongside kids of Eddie's age. From East Baltimore, these kids ran with fearlessness and a chip on their shoulder, their world steeped in the rough and tumble ways of street life.

My first run-in with the police was with these kids, and as the youngest and smallest, I was the low man on the totem pole. One of the kids in our "crew" was harassing a neighbor and pulled out a cap gun but pretended it was real. My heart never raced so much. When the cops came, we ran and hid under the porch.

I never thought I could be this scared. The first of many close calls. Whether it was standing up to a punch in the face or dishing one out, I always had to watch my back. It was an eat or be eaten type of mentality, 24 hours a day.

Then, one day, the energy in the group shifted. Still the youngest and smallest, the way the kids interacted with me was, let's just say, way less aggressive. So, I grew an inner confidence, attributing it to my own efforts until my dad let it slip. Eddie had confided in him that he told those kids if anyone messed with me, they would have to deal with him. In any other circumstance, such an action might have left me feeling inadequate, but not this time.

Eddie was my rock and my hero. Having him by my side was a relief, and because of him, I knew everything would be okay, and it always was. You know the saying, take a bullet for you? I do, because many times, it felt all too close and he never flinched. He was always there for me when the stakes were high.

How could I not worship the ground Eddie walked on? His essence and energy was palpable; when he walked into a room, everyone could feel it. His personality and presence were as big as his heart. He made everyone feel special. And he was an absolute warrior, a force to be reckoned with.

I wanted to be like Eddie in every way, except for maybe his questionable haircuts and odd sleeping patterns at times. But beyond that, in every way. He was the very best brother, showed me the ropes, and never left me behind. As he grew into a beast of a man, physically, mentally, and spiritually, he taught me how to make these quantum leaps, too.

A "bull in a China shop," Eddie never backed down from a challenge; and taught me how to do the same. I remember him taking me to Joseph Lee Park, full boxing gear in tow, to teach me how to fight. It's important to note that I never hit him once. And to this day after quite a bit of fighting, no one has ever hit me harder.

A perfect combination of strong and sweet, Eddie showed me tough love, never took it easy on me, and pushed me to reach the potential he saw in me. He saw me for who I was, which helped him shape and mold me into the person I am today. From the days with Eddie, I've always looked at my success as a team effort. Eddie came into my life at the perfect time to prepare me for the adversities I would encounter ahead.

And looking back, if he hadn't toughened me up at 13, exposing me to the trials and tribulations of the world, I would've gotten destroyed at Patterson High School. By the time I was a freshman, I had a been-there, done-that mentality that made every obstacle seem more like a small inconvenience.

Unless you come from this type of environment, it's difficult to truly understand what it really means when someone has your back. Eddie taught me loyalty and showed me what it felt like to have a ride or die, sit in traffic, or bury a body type of loyalty.

In addition to the rough and tough, take shit from no one attitude, Eddie had a sense of humor that often left me laughing so hard it hurt. Totally irritated by our constant debauchery, our parents would often separate us.

Eddie wasn't perfect, nor did he claim to be. As adults, we would reflect on our childhood. The more I listened, the more inspired I was by all he had overcome in his life. Eddie had a deep pain in his heart we could all feel, which is why no matter what he did, we all loved him anyway.

Always marching to his own beat, Eddie never quit and never gave up. Professionally he worked at the port, and he approached his work just as he did everything else: fully, all-in, and with an unwavering commitment.

My good friend, Rob Weinhold, once said, "When it's all said and done, what will you have said and done?" Although he left us suddenly and way too early, Eddie didn't hold back; he said and did it all. He made the most out of his life. God broke the mold with him; he was as unique as a thumbprint. Losing him was an emotional tsunami for me. My heart literally broke into a million pieces.

It took me some time to regain my ground and I'd be lying if I said my heart has mended itself. Truthfully, I'm not sure it ever will. Grief is a funny thing – it comes in waves, yet it's always there. It strips us down to our core, leaving us no choice but to move forward even when it seems impossible.

It reminds me of what my Dad said to me right before I walked down the aisle to marry my wife, Erica, "Forever is a long time, and nothing lasts forever."

Eddie's journey and his fearless embrace of life, with all its complexities and challenges, was a dance with infinity itself. His legacy inspires me to ask the deeper questions, to pursue truth relentlessly, and love myself and others fiercely.

Part 2: The Dance with Infinity

Speaking of forever, in the grand expanse of cosmic time, our tenure on this blue dot is but a fleeting moment. It's akin to a single heartbeat in the life of the universe – a brief flash of consciousness against the backdrop of an eternal void. And yet, within this brief moment, we possess the audacious capacity to question, to dream, and to seek understanding beyond the immediate grasp of our senses. We are infinite beings living in a finite world.

As Joe Rogan aptly put it: attempting to grasp the entirety of our existence is like trying to explain Netflix to an ant.[1] This vast disparity between our potential for comprehension and the actual scope of our understanding paints a picture of the human condition – our relentless pursuit of the unknown, driven by an inherent desire to unravel the mysteries of the universe.

Buzz Lightyear Had It Right, "To Infinity and Beyond!"

What, then, is infinity? This concept, as elusive as the furthest reaches of the universe, has puzzled the greatest minds throughout history. Despite our expanding knowledge – the universe's estimated width of 93 billion light years, the speed of light at 186,000 miles per second, the quantum realm's defiance of space and time – true comprehension remains just beyond our grasp.

And yet, the universe, in all its majestic indifference, provides a canvas for our most profound reflections. Amid this cosmic detachment, we discover our deepest purpose: to connect, to love, and to cherish each moment of awareness in this vast, infinite theater. It is not our physical size but our capacity to wonder and to seek truths beyond our sensory limits that truly defines us.

Rebecca Goldstein describes this journey beautifully: "That feeling of 'I am bigger because I know how small I am.'"[2] The realization that our significance is magnified by our awareness of our cosmic insignificance illuminates our innate wisdom and humility.

Naming the Unknowable: Dark Matter

In the cosmic sea, 93% remains hidden in the shadows of dark matter and dark energy, revealing that our understanding of the universe is but a mere fraction of its entirety.[3] This acknowledgment serves as a humbling reminder of our place within the cosmic order and highlights the profound truth of our existence: we know only a sliver of what exists and what is possible.

Dark matter symbolizes our attempt to chart the uncharted, to name the ineffable. Dark matter, alongside dark energy, forms the bulk of the universe's mass and energy, its presence not known through direct observation but inferred through the gravitational effects on the cosmos we can see.

As we find ourselves perched on the brink of cosmic discoveries, our journey from the known to the unknown is fraught with challenge and promise. The exploration of dark matter and dark energy is, yes, an academic pursuit but also a journey that questions the very foundation of physics and our understanding of the universe.

In this quest, we are reminded our place in the cosmos is defined by our willingness to seek, question, and marvel at the mysteries that remain. As we continue to peel back the layers of the unknown, let us move forward with humility and boundless curiosity, eager to uncover whatever secrets the universe may hold.

What's the Secret of the Universe?

Douglas Adams, in *The Hitchhiker's Guide to the Galaxy* (Del Rey, 2010), humorously suggests the answer to the ultimate question of life, the universe, and everything is simply *42*. Adams teases out the absurdity in our search for meaning within the vast, indifferent cosmos. He implies that perhaps the beauty of our quest lies not in finding definitive answers but in the journey of questioning itself.

The journey toward understanding the universe is much like wandering through a maze where each turn leads to new questions rather than clear directions. This endless maze, filled with wonders and mysteries like dark matter, quantum realms, and spacetime, shouldn't deter us but rather encourage us to dive in headfirst.

> "The universe is under no obligation to make sense to you."
> — *Neil deGrasse Tyson*

The Trap of Availability Bias

Our understanding of everything in our lives is invariably influenced by what is immediately known to us, a phenomenon known as *availability bias*. This cognitive shortcut often leads us to overvalue our knowledge and understanding, constrained as they are by the scope of our experiences and the breadth of our perceptions. Like trying to decipher the details of a label from within the jar, our perspective is inherently limited, rooted in the context of our existence within the vast cosmos. See Figure 9.1.

This limitation does not deter us but often emboldens us to form steadfast opinions about things we've never experienced. "I dislike that type of food" or "That doesn't make sense to me" are testaments to our preferences for certainty in the face of the unfamiliar.

Personally, I've experienced my own biases early in my career when it came to the idea that failure should be avoided at all costs. After multiple startup failures and a deep dive into the stories of successful entrepreneurs, I realized that failure is a critical component of innovation and growth. Much like a software update, we need

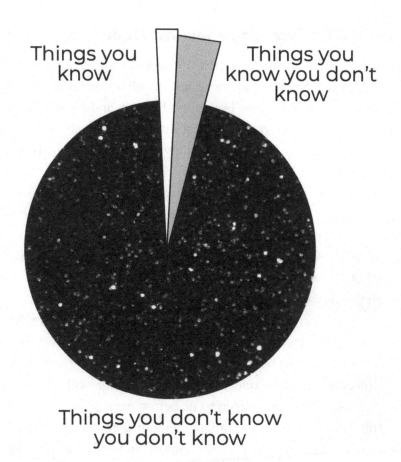

Things you know

Things you know you don't know

Things you don't know you don't know

Figure 9.1 Our limited perspective

human updates, too – revising and enhancing our perspectives with new information, new contexts, and new understandings.

> "Be patient toward all that is unsolved in your heart and try to love the questions themselves, like locked rooms and like books that are now written in a very foreign tongue. Do not now seek the answers, which cannot be given you because you would not be able to live them. And the point is, to live everything. Live the questions now."
>
> — *Rainer Maria Rilke*

203

What Say You?

When Did You Last Update Your Worldview Software?

When was the last time you took a moment to update your worldview software? Standing at the edge of what we know, we peer into the vast unknown with both apprehension and fascination. This is a direct challenge to our natural curiosity because we're much more comfortable in the arms of safety and security than we are in the unknown.

In order to move forward, we need to let go or quit our old world. Annie Duke's book, *Quit: The Power of Knowing When to Walk Away* (Portfolio, 2022) throws a wrench into the gears of our traditional views on letting go. She argues for the transformative power of knowing when to walk away, presenting quitting as not just an option but a strategic move toward personal growth.

Yet, how many of us have dismissed the idea of quitting without truly grappling with its implications or recognizing its value? Our societal and personal biases have often painted quitting in a negative light, revealing a wider reluctance to fully engage with and understand concepts that are foreign to us before we rush to judgment.

This habit of forming opinions without genuine understanding spills over into how we perceive power and influence in today's world. The "New Power" era, marked by its emphasis on collaborative, grassroots-driven change rather than top-down authority, challenges us to rethink leadership and participation.

Many resist this new paradigm mainly because of the lack of exposure to its dynamics and potential. The real task is for us to open our minds to alternative approaches to leadership and community building. Furthermore, our interaction with the natural world, as illustrated by Yuval Noah Harari's insights on the domestication of wheat in *Sapiens: A Brief History of Humankind* (Harper, 2015), encourages contemplation of whether we've truly mastered our environment or if, conversely, it has masterfully shaped us.

Much like our ancestors who believed they wielded control over wheat, we too often consider ourselves the definitive authors of our beliefs and ideas. Yet, the truth is our surroundings, our culture, and the ideas we encounter have a profound impact on shaping our perspectives and actions, often in ways we barely recognize.

In this journey of exploration and understanding, we are reminded that the act of learning and adapting is continuous. To truly navigate the complexities of our world and ourselves, we must remain open to revisiting and revising our beliefs, understanding growth lies not in the comfort of certainty but in the courage to question.

Put your seatbelt on because things have never moved so fast and will never move so slow again.

What We Can Learn from Dolphins

The 1994 University of Hawaii study on dolphin communication and behavior is a fascinating example of nonhuman intelligence and creativity.[4] In this study, researchers taught dolphins a unique form of sign language to communicate specific tasks.

The core of this study involved teaching dolphins two specific gestures. The first gesture was a command for the dolphins to "create" or "innovate" by performing an action they had not done before during their training sessions. This required the dolphins to remember all the actions they had previously performed and then conceive and execute a novel behavior in response to the gesture. This aspect of the study showcased the dolphins' remarkable cognitive abilities to understand abstract concepts, such as novelty and innovation, and apply their understanding in a creative manner.

The second, even more interesting, part of the study involved pairs of dolphins. Researchers instructed them, using a second gesture, to collaborate and create a new behavior together that neither had performed before in the study sessions. This required the dolphins not only to innovate but also to communicate effectively with each other, plan joint action, and synchronize their behavior to perform the new action simultaneously.

The fact that dolphins were able to understand these complex instructions and successfully create new, coordinated actions on the spot demonstrates their high level of cognitive function, social coordination, and communicative complexity. This behavior suggests dolphins have a sophisticated understanding of their own actions and the ability to communicate abstract concepts to each other, a trait once thought to be uniquely human.

If they can do it, so we can we.

This study's implications extend beyond marine biology, touching on themes relevant to AI development and human technology. It illustrates the potential for intelligence, whether biological or artificial, to exceed predefined limitations and innovate through collaboration. The dolphins' ability to innovate and work together in response to abstract concepts mirrors the potential for AI systems to collaborate with humans and with each other, creating solutions that are beyond the reach of individual entities. This parallel offers a compelling perspective on how combining diverse forms of intelligence – human, biological, and artificial – can lead to unprecedented levels of creativity and problem-solving.

Widening Our Circle of Concern

However, our current trajectory is marked by narrow optimization – prioritizing immediate gains over the collective good, leading to increased societal polarization and an erosion of shared reality. This approach is evident in the realm of social media and technology, where the race for dominance and attention has overshadowed the potential for AI to address global challenges.

The critique extends to the incentives driving technological development. Echoing the wisdom of Charlie Munger, who served as vice chair of Berkshire Hathaway, we recognize outcomes are deeply tied to incentives. The race among tech giants, fueled by profit motives rather than societal benefit, risks leading us toward a future filled with peril unless we realign these incentives toward the collective good.

In navigating this future, we should take a clue from the dolphins: to reconsider our approach to AI and technology by advocating for a model shift toward holistic well-being and collective problem-solving. This will take a concerted effort to realign our incentives and ensure technology serves as a force for good, enhancing human connection and fostering a more empathetic world.

The path we choose with AI and technology will significantly shape our future. By embracing a model of innovation inspired by the natural world and ensuring technology enhances our collective capacity for creativity, empathy, and connection, we can steer toward a future that reflects our highest aspirations for society and the planet. This narrative serves as a call to action, urging us to see beyond immediate challenges and envision a future where technology and nature, together, guide us toward a more authentic, connected, and innovative existence.

It's All Hard

You've likely come across the saying that resonates with the essence of life's inevitable hardships: Marriage is hard. Divorce is hard. Staying is hard. Leaving is hard. Life, in all its forms, presents challenges.

This core idea encapsulates what *Who Says?* aims to explore – if navigating life is inherently difficult, why not follow the path that resonates with your deepest truths? During a recent summer walk, I found myself in a conversation with my son, James, who was dealing with his own set of challenges at school.

"Choosing the easy path leads to a harder life while making the tough decisions often simplifies it," I explained. James's troubles stemmed from a classmate, "Biff," who embodied the quintessential school bully. Despite the discomfort, James was hesitant to speak up, fearing Biff's backlash.

Our conversation meandered to the importance of transparency and honesty, even when it led to uncomfortable conversations. I encouraged James to consider the broader implications of staying silent and shared with him the perspective that facing our fears, even when daunting, can lead to personal growth and resolution.

My wife Erica's "Do it scared" motto became our guiding principle, encouraging James to confront his situation head-on. This approach, which initially helped him overcome his reluctance to participate in flag football, now offered a pathway to address his current dilemma. After role-playing potential conversations, James decided to take the step forward, marking a significant moment of personal empowerment and bravery with his teacher.

To our greatest hope at that moment, James's decision to speak his truth to his teacher led to a positive outcome. She even wrote a letter to him and gave him such great acknowledgment of his courage and heart. He's got such gentle strength in this way. These are just two of the many things I admire greatly about our son, James.

This experience demonstrated a powerful lesson: life's success often hinges on our willingness to engage in difficult conversations and make hard choices.

Leading by Example in All Aspects of Life

The essence of leadership, whether in our personal lives or within our teams, lies in setting a precedent for courage, perseverance, and the willingness to tackle challenges head-on. There isn't a universal solution to life's difficulties, but by fostering an environment of openness, resilience, and innovation, we can guide those around us to face their own challenges with confidence and determination.

In the landscape of work and personal fulfillment, a few pioneering individuals and companies have carved paths that diverge from conventional wisdom. Take Patagonia, for instance. Annually, this trailblazing company pauses its operations between Christmas and New Year's, granting every employee a fully paid week off.

Their rationale is simple yet profound: "Our people need a break." Yvon Chouinard, the visionary behind Patagonia, encapsulates this ethos in his belief, "Every time I do the right thing, I make money."[5] This principle resonates deeply with me, highlighting a path where ethical practices align with business success.

Challenging the Status Quo

As society evolves, so too should our perceptions of work, success, and fulfillment. Here are some buried assumptions, agendas, and authorities worthy of a second look, offering opportunities for a richer, more adaptable approach to life and work:

- **Retirement at 65:** This benchmark, rooted in historical and policy contexts, might not fit everyone's needs or desires in today's world, where longevity and vitality extend well into later years. The choice between continuing to work or embracing early retirement is deeply personal, often driven by a blend of financial, health, and lifestyle considerations.

- **The 40-hour workweek:** Born from labor movement victories, the standard full-time workweek doesn't account for the vast diversity in job functions, individual productivity, or work-life balance preferences. The call for flexible hours, condensed workweeks, or tailored schedules speaks to a growing recognition that one size does not fit all.

- **The five-day workweek:** The traditional Monday to Friday routine is under scrutiny as evidence mounts that alternative schedules could enhance productivity and personal satisfaction. The emerging trends of remote work and compressed workweeks challenge this norm, advocating for a more nuanced understanding of how we allocate our time.

- **Climbing the corporate ladder:** Equating success with upward mobility within a company overlooks the value of lateral moves, specialization, or roles that prioritize satisfaction and impact over rank.

- **Job security and employer longevity:** The old adage that loyalty to a single employer ensures job security is increasingly outdated in a rapidly changing economic landscape. Today, adaptability, continuous learning, and flexibility are key to sustaining employability.

- **Separation of work and personal life:** Although maintaining boundaries is important, a rigid separation between professional and personal spheres might result in missed opportunities for integration that can lead to greater overall satisfaction and well-being.

- **The ideal of full-time employment:** This model often ignores the potential of part-time roles, freelancing, consulting, or entrepreneurship to provide fulfilling, flexible, and sometimes more lucrative work arrangements.

- **Success defined by material wealth:** This narrow view of achievement overlooks the significance of personal growth, social contribution, relationships, and other intangible yet deeply rewarding aspects of life.

By questioning these long-standing beliefs, we open the door to a more nuanced, whole, and personalized approach to work and life – one that values flexibility, personal fulfillment, and ethical engagement over adherence to outdated norms.

Making It Up, Moment by Moment

Navigating the uncharted waters of parenthood, each of us writes our own map as we go, often relying on instinct more than instruction. In one of my most memorable dad moments, our then 7-year-old daughter Ellie, with her insatiable curiosity, persistently inquired about the reality of Santa Claus. Embracing honesty, a value I've always aimed to uphold, my wife and I decided it was time to share the truth about Santa with her.

Weeks later, Ellie's curiosity hadn't waned, but this time, her questions ventured into territories I found myself unprepared for, topics I could barely recall or had never even considered. It was during one of these exchanges that I found myself at a loss, confronted with the infinite complexities of a child's curiosity and the limitations of my own knowledge.

Looking into her earnest, expectant eyes, I admitted, "Hey, I don't really know what I'm doing here. I've never been a dad before. Like, no idea. Sure, I've read books on parenting, but they only take you so far. I'm literally making this up, moment by moment."

"Making it up, moment by moment."

There was something liberating in that confession, a shared understanding that neither of us had all the answers.

Ellie, with her wise-beyond-her-years soul, seemed to grasp the profundity of this acknowledgment. She understood that life, in all its messy and glorious unpredictability, is a journey we navigate in real time, making decisions and forging paths with no certain guidebook.

This moment between us underscored a fundamental truth that extends far beyond the realms of parenthood: we are all, in essence, making it up as we go along. And we should be!

As we have learned through this narrative, if we rely solely on history and those who have come before to dictate how we live our lives and why, we are missing key pieces of innovation and self-discovery.

Whether it's facing the myriad challenges of raising children, navigating personal or professional dilemmas, or simply trying to make sense of the world around us, we proceed moment by moment, guided by a blend of wisdom, intuition, and the willingness to embrace the unknown.

In recognizing this, there's a profound sense of connection and humility that emerges – not just between parent and child, but among us all as fellow travelers on this unpredictable journey of life. It's a reminder that although the path may be unmarked and the outcomes uncertain, there's beauty and growth to be found in the very act of navigating it, step-by-step, together.

Now, as we stand at the precipice of tomorrow, armed with our dreams, curiosity, and the infinite paths before us, let's make a pact. To venture into the unknown with hearts wide open, to live fully into the questions of our lives, and to embrace the beautiful uncertainty of our existence with courage and grace.

Where will your next step take you? What Say You?

Epilogue: In Truth, In Love

Before you go, I am compelled to share one final insight, a profound realization that has become the North Star of my existence. Amid the humbling vastness of our unknowns, there emerges a singular, unshakeable truth that resonates within the deepest chambers of my soul: love is the ultimate truth, and truth, in its purest form, is love.

I've heard the line, "Before the truth sets you free, it tends to make you miserable."[1] This paradoxical wisdom encapsulates the transformative power of truth – it confronts us, challenges us, and ultimately liberates us, though not without first leading us through the valleys of introspection and discomfort. Yet, it is within these valleys that the most fertile grounds for growth and understanding are found.

My journey to this understanding has been profoundly shaped by my life's greatest teacher – my wife, Erica. She is my steadfast partner, my ride-or-die, my best friend, and the most divine expression of love I have known. She is my home. Together, we have navigated the complexities of life, love, and understanding, each lesson weaving us closer, each challenge strengthening our bond.

The path we've walked together has been rich with lessons of love, resilience, and the transformative power of truth. And, as we stand on the threshold of tomorrow, hand in hand, I am filled with a profound sense of gratitude and excitement for what lies ahead.

My heart swells with anticipation for the adventures that await us and our family.

Being here with her now, sharing this moment, this connection fills my heart whole. As we close this book and look toward the horizon, I am anchored by a hopeful anticipation. There's a sense, a feeling in the air that our next journey holds wonders yet to be discovered. I love you, baby.

So, as we part ways for now, my invitation for you is to carry forward with open hearts and minds, ready to embrace the truths that await us, grounded in love and propelled by the shared journey of our human experience. For it is in truth, in love, that we find our most authentic selves and the deepest connections to one another.

Until next time, may our paths be guided by love, our challenges tempered by understanding, and our lives enriched by the endless pursuit of truth.

Notes

History Is Happening

1. Before the pandemic, 70% of the workforce is not engaged. https://www.gallup.com/workplace/391922/employee-engagement-slump-continues.aspx
2. Although only 12% of executives believe their teams are productive, a staggering 87% of employees consider themselves highly productive. https://www.microsoft.com/en-us/worklab/beyond-the-binary-solving-the-hybrid-work-paradox

Introduction

1. In 1868, an American inventor, Christopher Latham Sholes, was granted the world's first patent for a typewriter. https://www.britannica.com/biography/Christopher-Latham-Sholes
2. This benchmark wasn't born out of consideration for human well-being or productivity. Its origins can be traced back to the turn of the 20th century in Germany. https://www.ssa.gov/history/age65.html
3. But the one that really fires me up, especially as the dad of a 13-year-old daughter and 11-year-old son is why we have school bells to tell kids when classes start and end. https://hackeducation.com/2022/01/30/bell
4. Seventy percent of us are not engaged. https://www.gallup.com/workplace/391922/employee-engagement-slump-continues.aspx
5. *Harvard Business Review* reported that 70% of change initiatives fail in organizations. https://hbr.org/2016/10/organizations-cant-change-if-leaders-cant-change-with-them#:~:text=In%20a%20survey%20of%20nearly,70%25%20of%20transformation%20efforts%20fail

6. Airbnb let their employees work from anywhere without adjusting pay as a thank-you for their contributions during the pandemic. https://news .airbnb.com/airbnbs-design-to-live-and-work-anywhere/#:~:text=To%20 recap%2C%20here%27s%20our%20design,and%20work%20around%20 the%20world

7. TowerPaddle Board has been working five-hour days for years now with great success. https://www.towerpaddleboards.com/blogs/pages/v-five-hour-work-htm

8. In 2017, Google published its findings from Project Aristotle, where it studied hundreds of teams to understand the main driver of a high-performing environment. https://www.nytimes.com/2016/02/28/magazine/what-google-learned-from-its-quest-to-build-the-perfect-team.html

Chapter 1

1. The Netflix documentary *Unknown: Cosmic Time Machine* shed light on our cosmic history and the incredible journey of this telescope. https://www.netflix.com/title/81473680

2. His research indicates the universe is double the age, approximately 26.7 billion years, we've been taught it was. https://www.openaccess government.org/age-of-universe-research-james-webb/163845/ #:~:text=Age%20of%20the%20universe%20estimated,estimate%20of%20 13.7%20billion%20years

3. Research by the Office of Economic Opportunity for NASA's Imaginative Thinking Test found we are 96% less creative as adults than we were as children. https://www.inc.com/rohini-venkatraman/4-ways-to-get-back-creativity-you-had-as-a-kid.html

4. The Baby-Jumping Festival (El Colacho) in Spain: This unusual tradition involves men dressed as devils jumping over infants to cleanse them of original sin. https://www.nationalgeographic.com/culture/article/el-colacho-baby-jumping-festival-murcia-spain#:~:text=In%20a%20heart% 2Dstopping%20display,protection%20from%20disease%20and%20 misfortune

5. The Bullet Ant Initiation in Brazil: The Satere-Mawe tribe in Brazil has a coming-of-age ritual involving young men wearing gloves filled with bullet ants, whose bites are among the most painful in the world. The purpose is to prove one's strength and endurance. https://www.acs.org/education/resources/highschool/chemmatters/past-issues/archive-2011-2012/yourbody.html#:~:text=The%20boys%20take%20part%20in,painful%20as%20a%20bee%20sting

6. The Aghori Sadhus in India: The Aghori are known for their extreme and unorthodox rituals, like meditating over corpses or consuming human remains, as a path to enlightenment. https://en.wikipedia.org/wiki/Aghori

7. The Tomatina Festival in Spain: In Buñol, Spain, participants engage in a massive tomato fight each year. Although it's a fun and popular event, most don't know its origins: it involved a spontaneous food fight among villagers in the 1940s. https://en.wikipedia.org/wiki/La_Tomatina

8. Firewalking in Greece: In some Greek Orthodox communities, many partake in the tradition of firewalking as a cultural tradition, with no understanding of it being an ancient practice with deep spiritual significance. https://www.nytimes.com/2021/02/01/travel/greece-firewalking-ritual.html

9. This unique experience, known as the *overview effect*, offers an entirely different perspective on earth. https://en.wikipedia.org/wiki/Overview_effect

10. Miki Agrawal is the author of the book *Disrupt-Her*. She is a serial entrepreneur who had already taken on several different industries and turned them on their heads before she reached the age of 40. https://mikiagrawal.com

11. A headline in *The Times* of London in 1894 announced that "in 50 years, every street in London will be buried under nine feet of manure." https://www.historic-uk.com/HistoryUK/HistoryofBritain/Great-Horse-Manure-Crisis-of-1894/#:~:text=By%20the%20late%201800s%2C%20large,under%20nine%20feet%20of%20manure

12. In his book *Enlightenment Now*, Steven Pinker points to the extraordinary progress that has been made in the last 200 years—exponential, relative to any other time period in recorded history. https://stevenpinker .com/publications/enlightenment-now-case-reason-science-humanism- and-progress

13. Compared to 200 years ago, 95% of the world no longer lives in poverty. https://www.economist.com/books-and-arts/2018/02/24/steven-pinkers- case-for-optimism

14. In *The Second Mountain*, David Brooks talks about how we as people try to climb the first mountain of fame and fortune, and if, or when, we get there, we realize the second mountain is about the fulfillment of purpose and impact and service. https://www.amazon.com/Second- Mountain-David-Brooks/dp/0812993268

15. Wurman, R. S. (2017). *UnderstandingUnderstanding* (Author).

Chapter 2

1. Back in the 1970s, people like Gregory Bateson and R. D. Lang researched what happens to people when they are presented with multiple confusing and conflicting narratives; much of their research based on families. https://www.edge.org/conversation/john_brockman-gregory-bateson- the-centennial

2. Stephen Cope's *The Great Work of Your Life* is a compelling exploration of finding one's true calling or *dharma*, as termed in the Bhagavad Gita, an ancient Indian scripture. https://www.amazon.com/Great-Work-Your- Life-Journey/dp/055380751X

3. It's time to think like Audrey Tang, Taiwan's trailblazing digital affairs minister. https://time.com/collection/time100-ai/6308288/audrey-tang/

4. Lynne Twist said once, "Look for the global problems that really upset you, that you think are unfair. There's a clue there. Look at the people you admire . . . the things that you have committed yourself to over and over again . . . What is your stand? Why were you born? What are you here for? What is your life really, really about?" https://www.eliseloehnen.com/ episodes/lynne-twist

5. Speaking of, *The Top Five Regrets of Dying* is one of my favorite all-time books. https://bronnieware.com/blog/regrets-of-the-dying/

6. In his book, *The Power of Regret*, Dan Pink highlights the transformative power of regret through the interesting story of Alfred Nobel. https://www.amazon.com/Power-Regret-Looking-Backward-Forward/dp/0735210659

Chapter 3

1. Despite the trillions of dollars pumped into companies to fix disengagement at work, 70% of people continue to go through their days without any sense of meaning or purpose. https://www.weforum.org/agenda/2016/11/70-of-employees-say-they-are-disengaged-at-work-heres-how-to-motivate-them/

2. In *Reinventing Organizations*, Frederic Laloux explores groundbreaking organizational models that challenge the traditional, hierarchical approach to power and leadership. https://www.reinventingorganizations.com

3. In *New Power* by Jeremy Heimans and Henry Timms, contrasts "new power" with "old power." https://www.amazon.com/New-Power-Works-Hyperconnected-World/dp/0385541112

4. Dr. Shefali Tsabary, a renowned expert in conscious parenting, writes about how many of us were raised in an authoritarian style of parenting, where we were expected to follow instructions without question. A typical interaction might go like this: https://www.drshefali.com

5. Psychologist Doug Brackman, author of *Driven*, suggested about 2% to 3% of the population can be clinically defined as psychopaths—people who have abnormally low empathy and are willing to cause harm to others in order to fulfill their own agenda (often involving power). Brackman suggested this small percentage of the population is not necessarily maleficent by choice; they are just hardwired toward an addiction to power. https://www.amazon.com/Driven-Understanding-Harnessing-Entrepreneurs-Athletes/dp/1619616939

6. Doug Brackman, *Driven*.

Notes

7. This phenomenon is rooted in the concept of learned helplessness, a theory put forward by psychologists Martin Seligman and Steven Maier in 1967 based on observations from their canine experiments. https://www.ncbi.nlm.nih.gov/pmc/articles/PMC4920136/#:~:text=Learned%20helplessness%2C%20the%20failure%20to,learning%20undermined%20trying%20to%20escape

8. Even today, after $1.4 trillion has been pumped into team building, consulting, and organizational development, many people will say, "I have a job," or "I'm looking for a job," instead of "I'm looking for an opportunity to fully express my gifts and allow my talents to shine." https://www.prnewswire.com/news-releases/smart-education-and-learning-market-to-reach-1-4-trillion-globally-by-2032-at-18-4-cagr-allied-market-research-301875349.html

9. Researchers like Daniel Goleman tell us that people who move through unpredictable situations really well make decisions not from a cognitive process in the prefrontal cortex but from a sense of *knowing,* which comes from the gut. https://www.bbc.com/worklife/article/20220401-intuition-when-is-it-right-to-trust-your-gut-instincts

10. Martin Seligman and his team at the Center for Positive Psychology at the University of Pennsylvania have measured well-being along 22 metrics. https://ppc.sas.upenn.edu/sites/default/files/wellbeingpublicpolicy.pdf

Chapter 4

1. Katie Hendricks, who has spoken and written extensively about personal sovereignty, calls this *authoring yourself.* Authoring yourself is about how you package yourself in the world, listen to and express your own creative juices, and share your purpose with the world. https://hendricks.com/about/our-story/

2. *Thinking Fast and Slow*, in which he names the various irrational shortcuts our brain takes to make sense of things; they create blind spots and can lead us astray. https://www.amazon.com/Thinking-Fast-Slow-Daniel-Kahneman/dp/0374533555

3. This kind of cognitive bias is also sometimes called the *Dunning-Kruger effect*, whereby "people with limited knowledge or competence in a given intellectual or social domain greatly overestimate their knowledge or competence in that domain relative to objective criteria or the performance of their peers, or people in general." https://lib.taftcollege.edu/c.php?g=861448&p=9266401#:~:text=Dunning%2DKruger%20effect%2C%20in%20psychology,people%20in%20general%20(Duignan)

4. For example, a recent poll conducted by Hartford Financial Services discovered 88% of poll respondents considered themselves "cautious drivers." https://moderndriver.org/driving-and-the-dunning-kruger-effect/

5. If 80% of a group were "above average," then that average would not be average.https://www.bbc.com/worklife/article/20220401-intuition-when-is-it-right-to-trust-your-gut-instincts

6. It also has a secondary meaning: "lacking in foresight or discernment, narrow in perspective and without concern for broader implications." https://www.merriam-webster.com/dictionary/myopic

7. In his book *Driven*, the psychologist Doug Brackman emphasizes how much this capacity to overemphasize what we think we know makes us short-sighted. "Humility is simply the capacity to be honest with oneself. It's an absence of pride." https://www.amazon.com/Driven-Understanding-Harnessing-Entrepreneurs-Athletes/dp/1619616939

8. Ken Wilber's concept of "holons" provides a fascinating lens through which to view this question. Each human being, or holon, is not merely an isolated entity but a part of a greater whole—a whole-on, embodying both wholeness and a part of a larger system. https://noelbell.net/ken-wilber-and-integral-theory/

9. I mentioned Google published the Project Aristotle Study in the Introduction to this book. https://www.nytimes.com/2016/02/28/magazine/what-google-learned-from-its-quest-to-build-the-perfect-team.html

10. The consequence of this way of thinking, whether in a personal relationship or an organization, is called the *drama triangle*, which was developed by Steven Karpman. https://en.wikipedia.org/wiki/Karpman_drama_triangle#:~:text=He%20defined%20three%20roles%20in,aspects%2C%20or%20faces%20of%20drama

11. The Pareto principle, commonly known as the 80/20 rule, suggests that a majority of outcomes are often produced by a minority of inputs. https://en.wikipedia.org/wiki/Pareto_principle

12. Although Frederick W. Taylor's efficiency studies in the early 1900s, including his work at Bethlehem Steel, did not specifically articulate the 80/20 rule, his focus on optimizing work processes and improving labor productivity laid foundational principles that align with maximizing efficiency. https://en.wikipedia.org/wiki/Scientific_management

13. The Flow Research Collective, led by pioneers like Steven Kotler and Rian Doris, focuses on the science of flow states—those optimal states of consciousness where we feel our best and perform our best. Kotler and Doris's work emphasizes the transformative potential of accessing flow, revealing it as a gateway to heightened creativity and performance. https://www.flowresearchcollective.com

14. Cal Newport sheds light on a common scenario: many professionals find themselves handling tasks 20% beyond their comfortable capacity. https://calnewport.com/what-would-happen-if-we-slowed-down/

15. Drs. John and Julie Gottman emphasize that you need a 5-to-1 ratio of appreciation to criticism to have a successful relationship with anyone, and you have to start with yourself. https://www.gottman.com/blog/the-magic-relationship-ratio-according-science/

Chapter 5

1. George Zimmer, the founder of Men's Wearhouse, was one of the first CEOs to take a stand in the late 1990s by establishing a 1 to 20 limit on the pay disparity between the lowest and highest-paid workers. https://www.glossy.co/podcasts/mens-wearhouses-george-zimmer-on-his-second-act-after-being-fired-i-didnt-just-ride-off-into-the-sunset/

2. A more recent example, but with a twist, is Dan Price of Gravity Payments. Price made headlines in 2015 when he announced he would slash his own salary from about $1 million to $70,000, and set $70,000 as the minimum salary for all his employees. https://www.cbsnews.com/news/dan-price-gravity-payments-ceo-70000-employee-minimum-wage/

3. Similar to the national debt in America—it simply cannot keep increasing forever. Back in 1929, the US owed $20 billion in Treasury bonds, or 16% of the GDP, which was already seen at the time as a problem without any solution in sight. https://www.pewresearch.org/short-reads/2023/02/14/facts-about-the-us-national-debt/

4. In 2023, that figure is $34 trillion, 125% of the GDP, and approximately 1,500 times what it was less than 100 years before. https://www.cnbc.com/2024/03/01/the-us-national-debt-is-rising-by-1-trillion-about-every-100-days.html

5. Reflecting on a century's shift, an article from the *Atlantic* notes that in 1910, about a third of the US population—38 million people—were deeply entrenched in agriculture. By 1950, this number had decreased to just 10%, and by 2010, it stood at a mere 2%, despite an exponential increase in food production. https://www.theatlantic.com/business/archive/2012/03/how-the-tractor-yes-the-tractor-explains-the-middle-class-crisis/254270/

6. Although acknowledging AI's potential to exacerbate existing inequalities initially, Professor Scott Galloway also sees it as a conduit for greater prosperity, driven by enhanced efficiency and innovation. His cautious yet optimistic perspective suggests that with strategic integration of AI, businesses can achieve more equitable and creative outcomes. https://www.nbforum.com/newsroom/events/nordic-business-forum-2023/scott-galloway-unpacking-the-ai-burst-and-current-market-conditions/

7. Through the Ethereum blockchain, ConstitutionDAO swiftly raised more than $40 million globally, with contributors receiving tokens that provided a stake in the collective's decision-making process and possible ownership of the historic document. https://www.npr.org/2021/11/19/1057211030/constitutiondao-constitution-auction-cryptocurrency

8. In Rick Rubin's book, *The Creative Act: A Way of Being*, he puts it beautifully: "Turning something from an idea into a reality can make it seem smaller. It changes from unearthly to earthly. The imagination has no limits. The physical world does. The work exists in both." https://www.amazon.com/-/es/Rick-Rubin/dp/0593652886

9. In his book *Counterfeit Gods: The Empty Promise of Money, Sex, and Power, and the Only Hope That Matters*, Timothy Keller presents a succinct history of the American dream. https://a.co/d/dCvAjNp

10. In his book, *Chasing the Scream: The First and Last Days of the War on Drugs*, Johann Hari reflects on the Rat Park experiment done in the 1960s. https://www.amazon.com/Chasing-Scream-Johann-Hari/dp/1408857820

Chapter 6

1. This conversation about the inherent personal nature of business and the indispensable roles of trust and authenticity continues to evolve, emphasized by findings from the 2023 Edelman Trust Barometer. https://www.edelman.com/trust/2023/trust-barometer

2. John's story echoes Henry David Thoreau's poignant words in Walden: "The cost of a thing is the amount of what I will call life, which is required to be exchanged for it, immediately or in the long run." https://en.wikipedia.org/wiki/Walden

3. A renowned author and investigator, Graham Hancock, challenges conventional historical narratives with his in-depth research. https://grahamhancock.com

4. This profound contemplation has gained unprecedented momentum, particularly in the wake of a groundbreaking report by the *New York Times* in July 2017. https://www.nytimes.com/2017/12/16/us/politics/pentagon-program-ufo-harry-reid.html

5. *Encounters: Experiences with Nonhuman Intelligences* by Diane Pasulka, a professor of religious studies, brings a scholarly perspective to the discussion of nonhuman life forms and UFO phenomena. https://a.co/d/aeVpPfd

Chapter 7

1. It's said (but not verified) that Upton Sinclair said, "it's hard to get a man to understand something when his salary depends on his not understanding it." https://www.goodreads.com/author/quotes/23510.Upton_Sinclair

Chapter 8

1. Research by the Flow Research Collective highlights that achieving flow can increase productivity by up to 500%. https://www.flowresearchcollective.com

2. The conversation about PTSD, historically limited to the experiences of combat veterans, expands significantly when we consider the insights of works like Bessel van der Kolk's *The Body Keeps the Score* and the profound reflections of Gabor Maté, prompting a reevaluation of trauma and its pervasive influence. https://www.ncbi.nlm.nih.gov/pmc/articles/PMC6164108/; https://journals.lww.com/jaapa/fulltext/2014/05000/posttraumatic_stress_disorder_in_combat_veterans.4.aspx

3. The insights provided by Aldous Huxley in *The Doors of Perception* merely hinted at the possibilities. Still, it was my firsthand experiences with MDMA and psilocybin that ushered in new unlocks of understanding and healing. https://thereader.mitpress.mit.edu/when-aldous-huxley-opened-the-doors-of-perception/

4. According to the 2023 National Veteran Suicide Prevention Annual Report released by the Department of Veterans Affairs, 17 veterans, on average, die by suicide each day in the United States. https://www.mentalhealth.va.gov/docs/data-sheets/2023/2023-National-Veteran-Suicide-Prevention-Annual-Report-FINAL-508.pdf

5. In MAPS' groundbreaking Phase 2 trials, 61% of participants no longer qualified for PTSD after just three sessions of MDMA-assisted therapy. https://maps.org/mdma/ptsd/

6. **Neuroplasticity enhancement:** Studies, including one published in Cell Reports in 2018, demonstrate that psychedelics like psilocybin can significantly increase neuroplasticity, suggesting a mechanism behind the therapeutic effects for mental health conditions. https://www.ncbi.nlm.nih.gov/pmc/articles/PMC6082376/

7. **Global decriminalization and legalization efforts:** As of 2021, Oregon became the first US state to legalize psilocybin for therapeutic use, and Denver became the first US city to decriminalize psilocybin in 2019. Internationally, Portugal decriminalized the possession of all drugs in

2001, focusing on treatment over punishment. https://www.ncbi.nlm
.nih.gov/pmc/articles/PMC5367557/

8. **Traditional use in spiritual and healing practices:** The Eleusinian Mysteries, an ancient Greek rite, are believed to have involved the ingestion of a psychoactive potion, kykeon, as early as 1500 BCE, highlighting the long-standing human relationship with psychedelic substances for spiritual exploration. https://journals.plos.org/plosone/article?id=10.1371/journal.pone.0211023

9. **Improvements in end-of-life anxiety:** A 2016 study published in the Journal of Psychopharmacology found a single dose of psilocybin significantly reduced anxiety and depression in cancer patients, with about 80% of participants showing sustained benefits six months after treatment. https://www.ncbi.nlm.nih.gov/pmc/articles/PMC9760680/

10. **Microdosing trends:** An observational study published in 2019 in *PLOS One* found participants who practiced microdosing reported improved mood, focus, and creativity, indicating a potential nontraditional use of psychedelics that warrants further research. https://www.ncbi.nlm.nih.gov/pmc/articles/PMC5001686/

11. **Economic impact on mental health treatment:** A 2020 analysis by the *Journal of Psychopharmacology* estimated psilocybin therapy could save the US health care system up to $16 billion annually by reducing the costs associated with mental health conditions like depression and PTSD. https://www.ncbi.nlm.nih.gov/pmc/articles/PMC5367557/

12. **Psychedelic-assisted psychotherapy training programs:** Institutions like the California Institute of Integral Studies have launched certification programs in psychedelic-assisted therapies, preparing mental health professionals for the integration of these treatments into clinical practices.https://www.ciis.edu/research-centers-and-initiatives/center-for-psychedelic-therapies-and-research

13. **Impact on creativity and problem-solving:** Historical accounts and anecdotal evidence suggest psychedelics can foster creative breakthroughs. A study in *Psychopharmacology* (2012) found low doses of mescaline significantly enhanced problem-solving abilities, offering

potential insights into the cognitive benefits of psychedelics. https://journals.sagepub.com/doi/10.2466/pr0.1966.19.1.211

14. Recent research by the World Health Organization found every $1 invested in scaling up treatment for common mental disorders such as depression and anxiety leads to a return of $4 in improved health and productivity. https://www.who.int/news/item/13-04-2016-investing-in-treatment-for-depression-and-anxiety-leads-to-fourfold-return

15. Steven Kottler and Rian Doris of the Flow Research Collective are the world's leading experts in flow—a state where one's sense of time dilates, productivity skyrockets, and creativity flourishes. Empirical data curated by the collective indicates individuals in flow can experience up to a 500% boost in productivity, with creativity rates doubling and learning speeds accelerating dramatically. https://www.flowresearchcollective.com/zero-to-dangerous/overview

Chapter 9

1. As Joe Rogan aptly put it: attempting to grasp the entirety of our existence is like trying to explain Netflix to an ant. https://youtu.be/YdLi7ryiGyY

2. Rebecca Goldstein describes this journey beautifully: "That feeling of 'I am bigger because I know how small I am.'" http://www.whatisitliketobeaphilosopher.com/rebecca-goldstein

3. In the cosmic sea, 93% remains hidden in the shadows of dark matter and dark energy, revealing that our understanding of the universe is but a mere fraction of its entirety. https://en.wikipedia.org/wiki/Dark_matter

4. The 1994 University of Hawaii study on dolphin communication and behavior is a fascinating example of nonhuman intelligence and creativity. https://pubmed.ncbi.nlm.nih.gov/8315399/

5. Their rationale is simple yet profound: "Our people need a break." Yvon Chouinard, the visionary behind Patagonia, encapsulates this ethos in his belief, "Every time I do the right thing, I make money." https://www.simonesmerilli.com/business/yvon-chouinard

Epilogue

1. I've heard the line, "Before the truth sets you free, it tends to make you miserable." https://www.goodreads.com/quotes/871172-before-the-truth-sets-you-free-it-tends-to-make

Winning the National Football Foundation and 1995 College Hall of Fame Athlete awards with my dad, Jim; Coach Roger Wrenn; and my stepmother, Rose.

With my rock, my dad.

Our wedding vow renewal, 2023 in Southern California.

My home – Ellie, me, Erica, and James.

I always looked up to my brother, Eddie.

Johns Hopkins University graduation in 1999 with my mom, Debbie.

One of my mom's modeling shots.

The last picture that was taken with my brother, Eddie, and sister, Marisa.

Acknowledgments

In crafting the acknowledgments for *Who Says?* I find myself navigating a tidal wave of gratitude, each wave a testament to the extraordinary individuals who've added so much value to my life and this book's creation. Their influence has guided me through both the challenges and successes of this journey.

To my parents, Jim and Rose, and in loving memory of my late mom, Debbie, your essence courses through every word I write. You've sculpted my character, nourished my spirit, and provided the unconditional love that forms the bedrock of my existence. Your sacrifices, love, and wisdom have been my guiding stars, illuminating my path in the darkest nights.

Eddie, my late brother and guardian spirit, your role in my life has been monumental. An OG with a heart a of a lion, you were my protector, confidant, and the epitome of strength. Our bond, forged in the streets and fires of shared experiences, has been my consistent source of courage and inspiration.

To Kim, Kylie, and Zoie, though Eddie's physical presence is missed, his spirit lives on in our collective journey home, and I vow to honor his legacy by being there for you, as he was for me.

Marisa, my sister, your resilience and compassion, especially during the trials of COVID, have left me in awe. Trey, your addition to our family has brought joy and strength. Together, you represent the enduring bond of family that no adversity can diminish.

To my soulmate, Erica, you are my home and the everything of my world. Your love has taught me the true essence of partnership and the transformative power of love. We are partners in this life. Together, we navigate life's infinite possibilities, our bond a model of hope and understanding.

Ellie and James, my beloved children, you are my greatest teachers. Ellie, your creative spirit and strength inspire me daily. James, your kindness and wisdom remind me of the pure joy of discovery. I love our family adventures and time together. Thank you for being patient with me these past few years.

A heartfelt thank you to my godparents, Aunt Jackie and Uncle Kenny, for your unwavering support and love. You've been a constant source of strength and encouragement.

To Mickey, Megan, Freddie, and baby Sophia, your presence in our lives brings unparalleled joy. Your journey enriches our family, and I cherish our shared moments.

To my SHIFT team, your dedication and support have been instrumental in my growth. It's been my deepest honor to ride with all of you.

To my chosen family, chief among them Derek and Melanie Coburn. It's been such a gift to raise our families together and adventure – along with the entire Cadre community, including Scott, Jere, Neal, Nema, Barry, Tim, Trey, Jenny, Jeff, and so many others, thank you.

To my other angel advisors, Nestor, Richard, Jeff, Shawn, Keith, and many others, your support means the world.

To my dear friends, Chris, Jason, Eliza, and the Guild of Great Men, thanks for always being there for me.

To Kelly, Craig, Jimi, Savana, Dr. Dan, Bayu, and Porangui, thank you for facilitating some of the hardest and best tender moments.

To Michael, my therapist, coach, and confidant, you have helped me see that I am enough. I can't put into words what that means to me and appreciate "who you be."

Cheryl from Wiley, your belief in this unconventional book has been a source of true partnership and validation. Your guidance has been invaluable in bringing this vision to life.

Krystina and Misti, your support, second eye, insights, and dedication have been crucial in shaping this book. Your contributions have elevated this project, and for that, I am eternally grateful.

To Arjuna, my early writing partner and friend. Thank you for putting all you had to give into this with me. I am grateful.

And finally, thank you to Mother Earth, the universe, and all that came before. As Ram Dass says, we are all just walking each other home – thank you times a million for making it this far in this journey together. Peace and Love.

About the Author

Joe Mechlinski is an award-winning business leader, entrepreneur, investor, speaker, and author. Joe's 2013 book, *Grow Regardless*, became a *New York Times* bestseller, followed by his second bestselling book, *Shift the Work*.

But this is far from where he started.

Joe grew up in Baltimore's inner city with food insecurity and intermittent, unstable housing. Miraculously, he went from the worst high school in Maryland to one of the most prestigious universities in the country (Johns Hopkins University). This changed the trajectory of his life, and eventually business. After attending 23 funerals by the time he was 23, he had to make a shift, or he wouldn't make it.

Today, Joe is the founder and CEO of SHIFT, a tech-enabled management consulting firm that has been nationally recognized as a nine-time "Best Workplace" by various business publications. He also launched an employee engagement platform, Latch, which uses artificial intelligence (AI) to help executive leaders to accelerate organizational change.

Joe is on a mission to change the way we work to transform the way we live. In 2022, Joe's TEDx Talk on this subject ranked number 40 most popular out of nearly 16,000 TEDx Talks. He helps leaders and organizations unblock, unlock, and unleash the potential and momentum of their people.

Beyond this, Joe has devoted his life to service, especially to his hometown of Baltimore. He is dedicated to helping underserved, at-risk communities and is a general partner with Conscious Venture Partners, a VC firm that invests in minority and female-founded businesses.

Captivating and inspiring audiences on national stages, Joe's passion is palpable – challenging the way people think, operate, and engage with themselves, relationships, life, and work.

Index

Page numbers followed by *f* refer to figures.

b4 students, 30

Blockchain, 125–126, 223n7

The Body Keeps the Score
(van der Kolk),
181, 225n2

Brackman, Doug, 71–72, 74–75,
96, 219n5, 221n7

Bridges, Ruby, 158

Bronner, David, 189

Brooks, David, 26, 218n14

Bullet Ant Initiation, 20, 217n5

Burns, Stan, 56, 135–136

Busyness, 48–49

C

Carey, Jim, 57

Carlin, George, 34

Center for Positive Psychology,
78, 220n10

Change initiatives, 6

Chasing the Scream (Hari),
128–129, 224n10

Cherry, Jeff, 56, 139

Chouinard, Yvon, 209, 227n5

Churchill, Winston, 123

Circle of concern, 206–207

Coburn, Derek, 56

Cocreation culture, 98–100, 99*f*

Cognitive biases, 220n2
authority bias, 116
availability bias, 95, 202–203,
203*f,* 221n3

and recognition of underdogs,
158–159
in thinking, 95

Collaboration, 18, 19, 98–100,
99*f,* 205–206

Competition, 147

"Complicated Conversations,"
168–169

Conscious parenting, 68–69

Conscious Ventures Lab/
Partnership, 139

ConstitutionDAO,
125–126, 223n7

Convention, questioning,
19–23. *See also*
Questioning
constructed reality

Convergent thinking, 17, 18*f*

Cope, Stephen, 46, 47, 218n2

Corporate responsibility, 138

Counterfeit Gods (Keller),
128, 224n9

COVID-19 pandemic, 5–7, 104,
179–180

Cowan, Joe, 155

Cowley, R. Adams, 112–113

The Creative Act (Rubin),
128, 223n8

Creative equity, 127–128

Creativity, 16
with artificial intelligence,
123–125

of children vs. adults, 17–19,
216n3
of dolphins, 205, 227n4
impact of psychedelics on,
185, 226–227n13
for sovereignty, 107
Criticism, 109, 222n15
Cruise, Tom, 118
Cryptocurrencies, 125–126, 223n7

D

Dark energy, 201, 227n3
Dark matter, 201, 227n3
Davis, Daryl, 159–161
Decca Recording Co., xi
Declaration of Independence,
120
Democracy, redefining, 161–162
Diamandis, Peter, 164
Disengagement, 63, 215n4,
219n1. *See also* Power
Disrupt-Her (Agrawal),
24, 217n10
Disruption, 11–32
in author's story, 12–15
history of, 25–26
by living with meaning and
purpose, 26–27
mindset for, 24–25
navigating a life of, 30–32, 31*f*
by questioning constructed
reality, 16–24, 27–30

Divergent thinking, 17, 18*f*
Doblin, Rick, 177–178
Dolphins, 205–206, 227n4
The Doors of Perception
(Huxley), 182, 187, 225n3
Doris, Rian, 107, 191,
222n13, 227n15
A Dose of Hope (Engle), 187
Drama triangle, 104–105, 221n10
Driven (Brackman), 71–72,
74–75, 96, 219n5, 221n7
Duell, Charles H., xi
Duke, Annie, 204
Dunbar, Robert, 98
Dunning-Kruger effect, 95, 221n3

E

Educational equity, 79–80
1883 (Sheridan), 54
Einstein, Albert, xi, 158
Eisenstein, Charles, 147
Eleusinian Mysteries, 184–185,
192, 226n8
Emerson, Ralph Waldo,
46–47, 46*f*
Encounters (Pasulka),
146–147, 224n5
End-of-life anxiety, 185, 226n9
Energy, elevating your, 107–108
Engagement, 63, 161–162, 177,
215n1, 215n4
Engle, Dan, 187

245

Index

250

Index